SPIRITUAL
WORKOUT
OF A
FORMER
SAINT

SPIRITUAL WORKOUT

OF A FORMER SAINT

DANNY ABRAMOWICZ

OUR SUNDAY VISITOR PUBLISHING DIVISION
OUR SUNDAY VISITOR, INC.
HUNTINGTON, INDIANA 46750

This book is dedicated to:

- Paper (my father) and Pepper (my father-in-law)
- Milton (my son-in-law's father)
- DJ and Andy (my sons)
- Joe (my brother) and Joey (my nephew)
- Stephen (my son-in-law)
- And last, but not least, Dillon (my grandson)

Contents

Preface

First, a Confession

I am nothing but a "has-been" football player and a fired ex-NFL coach. I was and still am a sinner who struggles daily to overcome my weaknesses. I have been a recovering alcoholic for 22 years. In other words, I have been "a lost ball in high weeds."

In spite of all that, I am living proof that God can change the life of anyone if we allow Him. If God can turn my sinful life around, any person has a chance, no matter what the condition of one's spiritual life is right now. God not only turned my life around, but also, through the working of His Holy Spirit, inspired and directed me in the writing of this book.

A Problem That Needs a Solution

In 1995, I began to notice that spiritual atrophy was settling into men's hearts, affecting the virtues of faith, hope, and charity. This spiritual atrophy could be noticed by the small numbers of men in attendance at Sunday Mass. It seemed to me that a growing number of men looked at spirituality as a sign of weakness and thought of it as something that was of interest only to women.

In general, men think their primary responsibility is to provide material support to the family. Sadly, what has happened is that men have shunned their duty as spiritual head of the family. In many families, the mother has taken over this obligation along with all of her other duties. Women, by and large, are holding up their end of the bargain, but men have dropped the ball.

All of this began to weigh heavily on my heart, so I began to pray fervently to the Holy Spirit, asking Him to help me touch men inwardly and to change their hearts. I felt that I had something special to offer. Through much of my life, I experienced all that seemed to be wrong with men today, and — thanks be to God — He lifted me up from that mess. I also believed that I would be able to relate to a wide variety of men because of my background in sports. I was convinced that it was time for men to get back into spiritual shape. And who would be better at accomplishing this task than our own Personal Trainer — namely, the Holy Spirit?

I continued to pray about this situation before the Blessed Sacrament in the adoration chapel at Marytown, a Conventual Franciscan friary located just outside Chicago, in a town called Libertyville, Illinois. The Holy Spirit began to unfold His plan to me, a plan utilizing athletic and workout terminology. Since it dealt with sports terminology, I called it the "spiritual fitness workout." I formulated a broad outline, which I used over the next several years as I began to travel around the country, speaking at Catholic men's conferences on this subject. Even as I was giving these talks, I was also incorporating the spiritual fitness workouts into my personal life.

Over this period of time, in giving these talks, I began to notice that men were relating to the message. In fact, they began asking me if I had published a book about these workouts. Of course, I had to tell them that I had not. Consequently, many of the men began to encourage me to write a book.

How This Book Came About

I began to pray to my Personal Trainer, the Holy Spirit, about a possible book. One day in my office, I was glancing at the newspaper and suddenly by chance (or the prompting of my Personal Trainer) I came across an article announcing that a national publishing convention was currently in town at the New Orleans Morial Convention Center. So I called a friend of mine, Jimmy Fore, who is the general manager of the convention center, and asked him if I could obtain a pass to attend the convention that afternoon. He called back a few minutes later and told me where to pick up the pass.

While driving over to the convention center, I placed this challenge before the Holy Spirit: "Lord, if You want me to write this book, I want You to connect me with a Catholic publisher this afternoon."

Upon entering this gigantic convention, I did not have the slightest idea where to begin looking for a publisher. For several hours, I wandered around the exhibits but found nothing. Becoming discouraged, I was about to leave, when all of a sudden I was standing in front of a well-known Catholic publisher's exhibit. I could not believe my eyes. I walked up to the person manning the booth, introduced myself, and began to tell him my story about the book. I gave him a copy of my broad outline and a business card.

Approximately two weeks later, I received a phone call from the president of this publishing house. He indicated that they were interested in talking to me about a book for men on spiritual fitness workouts. He suggested that I contact a priest-friend of his in Toronto, to help me with the editing. So Father Mike and I began working together — and even though we have never met in person, we have established a wonderful relationship, thanks to the benefits of this electronic age!

Several months went by, and we were making some decent progress with the first draft. I e-mailed the draft copy to the president for his evaluation. That's when I met my first obstacle in publishing this book. The publishing company never responded, so I assumed that they were no longer interested in producing my book. It bothered me for a short while, but I decided to move on.

A friend of mine advised me to contact another publisher, which I did, but the result was the same. They were not interested in a book that was strictly geared toward men.

Finally, I prayed to my Personal Trainer: "Okay! I am going to leave this in Your hands. If You want this book published, then send someone to me. If I don't hear from anyone, I will assume that I am not supposed to move forward with this book."

The Holy Spirit Takes Over the Project

Approximately a week later, after Mass at St. Joseph's Abbey, a beautiful Benedictine monastery located just outside of New Orleans, I ran into a friend of mine, Patti Mansfield. She asked me how the book was progressing, and I shared with her all that had happened. She began to share with me that during her prayer time she had "received a word," and that word was that I should contact Our Sunday Visitor about publishing the book.

Shortly afterward, I was speaking on the phone to another friend, Raymond Arroyo. During our conversation, he asked me how the book was coming along, and I shared with him my disappointment. Raymond immediately said that he had a friend at Our Sunday Visitor, and that he was going to call his friend and have him contact me.

When Raymond finished saying that, my jaw dropped and I thought most of my store-bought teeth would fall out of my mouth. A few days after that, I received a call from Our Sunday Visitor, and they asked me if I would e-mail a copy of the manuscript to them. Once they had a chance to review the contents, they said that they would be in touch with me.

Our Sunday Visitor Publishing not only called me back, but the editor who read the manuscript, Michael Dubruiel, said that he had been looking for something exactly like this and felt it was an answer to a prayer. He added that Our Sunday Visitor was excited about the possibility of publishing a book by me for men.

Now in Your Hands

My challenge to you as you begin to read this book is to consider this verse from St. Paul's letter to the Colossians:

QUOTE

Persevere in the *faith*, firmly grounded, stable, and not shifting from the *hope* of the gospel that you heard.

COLOSSIANS 1:23, emphasis added

Likewise, embrace the sentiments of this passage:

QUOTE

[I wish] that their hearts may be encouraged as they are brought together in love, to have all the richness of fully assured understanding, for the knowledge of the mystery of God, Christ, in whom are hidden all the treasures of wisdom and knowledge.

COLOSSIANS 2:2

May you find this *Spiritual Workout* beneficial in reaching your goal to become a strong and faithful disciple of our Lord Jesus Christ.

Introduction

From Lowly Beginnings to the
National Football League

Since the time I was a kid growing up in Steubenville, Ohio, I have always been a person who physically worked out. Early in my childhood, I would spend endless hours practicing football or playing baseball at North End Field. In the winter, I would go to the Catholic Community Center on Fourth Street and shoot baskets. These workouts didn't have any real structure to them. I would simply run, jump, kick, bat, catch, throw, and shoot.

In fact, I can even remember my younger brother Joe and I going to the railroad tracks, where he would pitch rocks to me and I would hit them with a baseball bat. It is utterly amazing that neither one of us was seriously injured with one of those flying rocks. I guess the good Lord was looking after us.

I must confess that my brother would get very mad at me, because I would always convince him to let me, his big brother, bat first, but when it was his turn at bat, I would say to him, "Mom's calling. It's time to go home." (There were some other occasions when I played dirty tricks on my brother, but I'm afraid to mention them here because my 84-year-old dad might read this book!)

Finally, around the sixth grade, I began participating in organized sports at St. Peter Grade School. St. Peter's Fighting Irish football, basketball, and baseball games spanned the school year, and Little League baseball filled the summer months. Many of the kids in my hometown were involved in athletics. I think people who live in steel-mill and coal-mining towns, such as Steubenville, love athletics and encourage their children to participate in sports.

My high school days were also filled with plenty of athletic activities. Most of the activities were organized sports requiring a tremendous amount of practice time. As I devoted more and more time to sharpening the various skills for each sport, I noticed myself improving in every sport.

Now, I must admit that God gave me some athletic ability, especially in the area of catching a football. I remember the first time I played catch with a football at the playground, catching it with my hands, even though I used an unorthodox method. Because of the success that I had in my junior and senior years in high school, I earned a football scholarship to Xavier University in Cincinnati.

For the first time in my athletic career, I was being paid to play a sport. At Xavier, many of our activities involving football were structured workouts, but I can remember spending a great deal of my personal time doing additional physical workouts. During my junior year, I was introduced to two new sports — handball and weightlifting. I was told that both of these activities would enhance my football skills. Through all the various physical workouts I was involved with, I noticed myself becoming bigger and stronger. By the time I was ready to graduate from college, I had increased my weight from 155 to 190 pounds.

The next thing that happened to me in athletics was one of the most exciting things that could possibly happen to a young football player. In the spring of 1967, my senior year in college, I was selected in the 17th round of the NFL draft by the New Orleans Saints. The Saints that year had become the most recent expansion team to enter the NFL. Since the 17th round was the very last round in the draft, I decided that I needed to work out harder than I ever had in my life, because I knew that when I reported to training camp, the coaches would be dreaming up various ways to cut me from the roster. I can tell you that I did work out harder and with more dedication and intensity than ever before in my life. I think that a lot of my drive came from the fact that deep down inside of me I wanted to prove them wrong for selecting me in such a late round.

That summer I reported to training camp in San Diego, in the best physical condition of my life. I knew that I had just one chance of making the team, and that it was a long shot. On the very day I stepped foot on the practice field, I suddenly realized that I was about to compete at one of the highest levels of competition there is in the world — the NFL. But as I began to take part in the grueling two-a-day practices, with all the running and vicious contact, it suddenly dawned on me that I was prepared to handle all of this because of the many conditioning workouts I struggled through, preparing myself for this opportunity.

Through the grace of God and hard work, I eventually made the Saints team that year. About midway through the season, due to another player's unfortunate injury, I was afforded the opportunity to start a game as wide receiver. I ended up having the game of my life, catching 12 passes against the Pittsburgh Steelers, and I remained a starter for the next eight years.

During those eight years in the NFL, I ended up having a very productive career. The key to my continued success and, for the most part, injury-free career was the physical workouts I pushed myself through during the off-season, preparing my body to endure the physical struggles of a long NFL season.

The reason I want to share all of this with you is not to inform you of my accomplishments, but rather to show you what can happen to people if they dedicate themselves to a physical workout program and stick with it over the long haul. It is utterly amazing what the human body can endure and accomplish. Take my advice and begin your own physical workout program and see for yourself the benefits that can come from discipline and sustained work.

Physical Well-being Isn't Just for Men

For all of you ladies, there is hope! My wife of 35 years would not listen to me in the least bit when I would try to encourage (force?) her to get involved in some kind of workout program. (Does this sound familiar, men?) Finally, one day several years ago, my wife informed me that she wanted to start a physical workout program. After I picked myself up off the ground, I told her that I thought it was a wonderful idea. I asked her if she would be open to two suggestions. She said that she might agree with my suggestions, once she heard what they were.

The first suggestion I made was for her to arrange for a physical exam with her doctor. Once she had clearance from her doctor, then I recommended that she contact a personal trainer to help her get started and guide her through this total workout process. It is utterly amazing how God's hand can intervene in all kinds of situations: My wife agreed to both suggestions. I am so proud of her progress and accomplishments. In fact, she recently ran the Crescent City Classic, which is a 10K race held each year in New Orleans.

Through her commitment to these workouts over the past two years, I can see a significant change in her, both physically and psychologically. She has actually dropped several dress sizes, and her entire outlook about the way she looks and feels is upbeat.

Her involvement in physical activities has added a new dimension to our marriage as well. Before she began her workout program, we were limited to the things we could do together. Most of our activities were of the passive nature, such as movies, the symphony, and dinner, just to name a few. But now we participate together in active ventures such as walking, hiking, jogging, and biking — as long as *my* knees hold out! As a result of incorporating active and passive interests, we now enjoy much more variety in our life together.

Another wonderful advantage of my wife's involvement in a physical workout program is that we have totally changed our eating habits. Through the advice of her personal trainer, she now puts together healthy and nutritious menus for the week. I never dreamed in a million years that I would be eating some of these vegetarian meals. I find some of them absolutely horrible, but by and large most of them are very good. By watching our diets, each of us has noticed a marked improvement in both our cholesterol counts and blood pressure. Don't get me wrong: We both still cheat and sneak ice cream and Reese's peanut butter cups occasionally. And when you live in New Orleans, which has a reputation for famous Southern-style cooking, you can only watch your diet to a certain extent. If you are offered an oyster po-boy or a plate of shrimp Creole with French bread and a piece of pecan pie for dessert, how can you turn them down?

Because we work out three to four times a week, we are able to cheat once in a while. But whenever we get away from our workout routine and stop eating healthfully for any length of time, there is always a price to pay. All we have to do is try on our clothes or jump on the scale to see the unpleasant results of our neglect. Taking proper care of the physical part of our bodies is important — and to do so successfully, as you can see, requires a tremendous commitment of both time and effort. I am a firm believer in this philosophy, especially because Scripture says that our body is a temple of the Holy Spirit.

QUOTE

Do you not know that your body is a temple of the holy Spirit within you, whom you have from God, and that you are not your own? For you have been purchased at a price. Therefore, glorify God in your body.

1 CORINTHIANS 6:19-20

My Spiritual Life

Just as my wife needed some prodding from me to take her physical life seriously, so did I when it came to my spiritual life. As I was growing up, for the most part, the spiritual aspect of my life and the physical part of my life that I just spoke of earlier mirrored each other in the exercise of the basic fundamentals of each. It wasn't until I entered the young-adult stage of my life that the physical and spiritual took opposite courses. Now, let's examine the spiritual part of my life.

My family, other relatives, and most of my friends in Steubenville were raised as Roman Catholics. Priests and religious played a major role in the formation of my Catholic faith and education. My parents were practicing Catholics, and they saw to it that my brother and I attended Mass each Sunday *with them*. We also received the Holy Eucharist when we came of age. At times, this was difficult because we were not permitted to receive Holy Communion unless we fasted after midnight. Then the Church changed the rule to no food for six hours before receiving Communion, and then the rule was changed to three hours, and now it is one hour before receiving Communion.

However, my personal prayer life was not much to speak of. Basically, it consisted of kneeling down and reciting a short evening prayer before going to bed. The majority of my praying took place at school, and this was vigorously "encouraged" by the Dominican Sisters who taught us.

During my high school years, we didn't pray nearly as much as we did in grade school. Personally, I only would say prayers either when I was in trouble or when I needed something. One other thing I remember about those days is the number of times I went to confession. The sisters had us so scared about going to hell that I wore out a path going to the confessional box. And I really became a pro at disguising my voice.

But, all in all, I must say that the priests, the sisters, and my parents provided me with a solid spiritual foundation in my formative years.

College Years

When I went away to college, my spiritual life decreased, while my physical and social activities increased. One thing to my credit, I must say, is that I continued attending Sunday Mass, and on occasion I would participate in a weekday Mass — especially if I had a major test that day and hadn't studied for it.

However, the basic fundamentals — such as prayer, confession, and the Eucharist, which were drilled into me during my childhood — were not practiced during my college years. During this period of my life and for almost the next 15 years, I was very lax in my spiritual exercising. This lack of spiritual fitness eventually caused a tremendous amount of disruption and chaos in my life and consequently in my family.

After college, as I pursued my career in the NFL, the more success and notoriety that came my way, the less time and attention I allotted to my spiritual life. In fact, living a lifestyle in the "fast lane" made it easier to fall into the temptation of sin. Added to all of this was an addiction to alcohol, which made it easier to anesthetize my guilt.

My conduct placed a tremendous strain on my marriage. I remember waking up in the morning with a hangover, telling my wife that I was sorry, and promising her that I wouldn't do it again. And lo and behold, sometimes I would be back at it again the very next day. This behavior continued even after I retired from football. My wife was at her wit's end with me. So she, along with some of her friends, began to pray that God would intervene in my life.

Turning Point

One morning I woke up — after a night on the town again — but something seemed different about this particular morning. Getting out of bed, I looked at my wife, who was sleeping, and then I walked softly into each of the three children's bedrooms, watching them as they slept. Going back to my bathroom, preparing to shave, I looked into the mirror, straight into my eyes, down into my soul. I said to myself: "I hate this person. And if this is the kind of life I am going to live, then life isn't worth living." I had lost all respect for myself, and I was at the bottom of the barrel. Here I was: a man that the world thought had it all together — a former NFL All-Pro player and an executive in the business world with all the perks. Wrong! I was miserable. I was a lost ball in the high weeds.

I really didn't know what to do. So I called a Jesuit priest-friend of mine, Tom Cronin, and told him that I needed to see him.

"What about later in the week?" he said.

"You don't understand, Padre," I replied. "I need to see you right now."

"C'mon over."

To make a long story short, Father Tom referred me to his friend Buzzy, who was the executive director of an alcohol and drug treatment facility in New Orleans.

Arriving at the facility, I went to the front desk and asked for Buzzy. I told them that I was there to talk to Buzzy about another patient, and that it wasn't concerning me. Finally, I was able to sit down and talk to Buzzy about my situation. He asked me to fill out a short questionnaire. After a few minutes, I stopped and asked him the reason for doing this. He replied, "Usually when a person answers 'Yes' to two or more of these questions, they are pretty well on their way to becoming an alcoholic." I had answered "Yes" to 14 out of the first 15 questions. My only "No" answer was to the question "Have you ever attended an AA meeting?"

Buzzy turned to me and asked if I would attend an AA meeting with him that night. Before I knew what was happening — as though someone else inside me was answering — I said, "Yes."

I went home and told my wife that I was going to attend an AA meeting that evening, and I asked her if she would attend an Al-Anon meeting at the same time and place. (Al-Anon is a support group for relatives, friends, or loved ones of alcoholics.) Telling her that I knew she was fed up with all my broken promises, I said that I was going to AA not for anyone else but for myself, and that I wasn't going to *talk* anymore: I was going to *act*. She did attend that meeting and several others after that.

And so, on December 15, 1981, I attended my first AA meeting. I have the disease of alcoholism.

Some people reading this book might be saying, "Poor Danny." It's not "poor" Danny; it's *lucky* Danny, *blessed* Danny! The disease of alcoholism was the best thing that ever could have happened to me, because God used it to get my attention.

I was not a happy camper in the early weeks of attending these meetings. I was filled with all kinds of emotions, especially anger and feeling sorry for myself. But I kept going back and attending meetings, one day at a time. As a result, I was becoming sober, but not serene.

I began to experience an inward nudging that began to stir my interest in the spiritual side of my life. In fact, one day I was reading the newspaper in the backyard when suddenly the wind blew the paper open to a page that had an advertisement for an upcoming Catholic Bible study at St. Rose of Lima Church. The next thing I knew, I found myself sitting in an old classroom filled with a bunch of ladies and nuns, with one other man.

The first time the instructor asked us to open our Bibles to Ephesians, I thought he was talking about a linebacker. There was a loud crackling sound when I opened my brand-new Bible, which made everyone turn around and look at me. I told them that I had just purchased this new Bible because I wore out my first one.

After several weeks in this Bible study, the teacher, Benny Suhor, stopped me after class and invited me to a prayer meeting at St. Benilde Church. And once again — as though somebody else inside me was answering — before I knew what was happening, I said that I would attend. As I got into my car, I was so aggravated at myself for saying yes.

The following Wednesday, I attended this prayer meeting — and I made sure that I sat in the very last row next to the wall. A few minutes later, two huge ladies, with Bibles and umbrellas and everything else you could think of, came in and sat next to me in my pew. The prayer meeting began several minutes later, with more singing than I had ever heard at any Catholic function in my life. Everyone was standing and singing. Finally, the music stopped, and a noise rose from the group that sounded like a bunch of bumblebees. The leader explained that they were praying in tongues. All I knew was that I wanted to get the hell out of that place, but I was trapped by those two ladies.

All of the people had their eyes closed. So I began looking around, and much to my surprise they all had smiles on their faces, as opposed to the frown on mine. I said to myself, "That's what I want." When the prayer meeting ended, it seemed as though I couldn't get out of that place fast enough. But guess who was waiting outside for me? You guessed it: Benny! He said to me, "Brother, next Wednesday they are going to begin a Life in the Spirit Seminar." Benny said that he thought it would be a good idea for me to attend this seminar. Before I knew it — again, as though someone else was answering for me — I said yes. When I walked away, I couldn't have been more aggravated at myself for agreeing to go. But there I was, the following Wednesday, sitting in a Life in the Spirit Seminar.

For those not familiar with a Life in the Spirit Seminar, it is a series of lectures explaining how to allow the Holy Spirit to work in our lives. The seminar usually lasts seven sessions. I couldn't believe I was still there for the fifth session!

Spiritual Transformation

In this particular session, the instructor drew three circles on the board, and he explained that these circles represent all of the individual people in the world. He went on to say that the first circle has a cross just outside of it. The second circle has a cross just inside of it. The third circle has a cross in the middle. He said that this cross represents Jesus Christ and His relationship to us in our lives.

The instructor started by saying that the first circle represents a person that has the Lord nowhere in his life. I couldn't relate to that person because I did have the Lord in my life.

The second circle, he said, is a person that has the Lord in his life, but that the center of his life could be power or money, and that everything else — including God — revolves around that. As I started to reflect on my past life, I realized that I had made my ego and booze the center of my life, and that my job, my family, and my God revolved around me.

Finally, he said that the third person is one that has Jesus Christ at the center of his life. His job, his family, and everything that he does must revolve around God. When I heard that, I suddenly realized that this was what had been missing in my life. God was not the highest priority in my life. All sorts of other secular things came first for me. I knew that I had to make Jesus Christ the center of my life, the Master and King of my life, and that I must turn everything over to Him. I suddenly realized that He wanted me to accomplish all of the things that I had done in my life — but for *His* glory, not mine. That evening, I asked the Lord, in prayer, to come into my life as the center of my life, and to change my heart. From that moment on, my life has never been the same.

You see, men, our heart has a funny door that leads to it. It only has a handle on the inside, and we must open it and allow Jesus to enter in. Once I invited Him to come into my heart in a deeper way, my life began to change dramatically. "I" left my life and "We" entered in. Up to this point, I was more concerned about what was in it for me. Now I was more interested in others than in myself. Love entered my heart, and the anger and resentment and confusion began to leave. Love and anger cannot abide at the same time. Love will overcome. My change of heart was very noticeable in all of my relationships, especially the ones with my immediate family.

One thing I must mention here: Just because you turn your life over to the Lord, that doesn't mean that everything is going to be all peaches and cream. In fact, in many instances, like mine, things get worse before they get better. This is a long-term process in which the Holy Spirit begins working to change the various flaws in our human nature, and the devil puts up resistance every step of the way. Also, during my drinking days, I had made some horrendous mistakes by getting involved with investments that went completely under. As a result of these poor financial decisions, I lost our home and created a tremendous amount of debt, which created a lot of anxiety and guilt in me, and placed my family in a very precarious position. Even though I knew my family loved me and that they were not holding me totally responsible, I still felt a deep sense of guilt.

Around the same time that all of this was happening, the Lord spoke to me inwardly about starting a Catholic men's prayer group at my house. I thought, "Lord, you must be joking. Here I am trying to work an AA program, dig myself out of tons of debt, and deal with a case of the guilts, and You want me to start a prayer meeting at my home that I have up for sale. Excuse me . . . I mean the home that the *bank* has up for sale."

Each time I reflected on this and tried to ignore this calling, the more the answer came back: "Yes, I want you to start this Catholic men's group, and I want you to start it NOW."

Finally, I got the message and decided to invite 12 men to my home, some of whom I hardly knew. Then a strange thing happened. Every single man that I invited said that he was interested, and each one of them showed up the first night. None of us really knew what to do, except to begin to pray that God would reveal His plan for us.

The more we met and prayed, the more our group increased. Most of the men I had never laid eyes on before in my life. This group began taking on the charisma of praise, worship, and sharing. This men's prayer group was exactly what I needed at this time in my life. After approximately two years of not being able to sell the house and the group having grown to such a large number (90), we finally discerned that God wanted us to move the meeting to a larger facility. So, not long after the decision had been made to move the meeting to a larger facility, we sold the house — and that made the bank very happy.

It is by the grace of God that the Monday Night Disciples prayer group is still going strong after 18 years. Currently, we have two separate meetings in New Orleans, with a core group of about 20 to 25 men in each group. The hour-and-a-half meetings are held each Monday night, starting at 7:30.

After I completed the Life in the Spirit Seminar, I attended two Spiritual Growth Seminars, which really enhanced my understanding of the Scriptures and how to apply them to my daily life. These seminars also gave me a greater appreciation of the sacramental beauty of the Catholic Church. The fruits of these spiritual-training seminars included an increased awareness of the importance of prayer in my life and a desire to attend Mass more frequently during the week. I also became aware of the value of utilizing the Sacrament of Reconciliation more often.

By the grace of God and the prompting of my Personal Trainer, the Holy Spirit, since the late 1980s I have attended daily Mass, prayed daily, and gone to confession monthly. (Regarding the latter, my wife has just interjected something, saying that I should add the phrase "more frequently if necessary." I've thanked her for her wonderful insight!)

I am not making you aware of these changes in my life to make you think that I am "holier than thou." That is the furthest thing from what I am trying to get across. I just want you to know that if God can change my life around, away from the lifestyle I was living, then I think anybody has a chance of having his life changed, *if he really wants to* and *if he is open to the prompting of the Holy Spirit, our Personal Trainer.*

Get the Holy Spirit as Your Personal Trainer

Personal Trainers

The dictionary describes a physical, or athletic, trainer as a person that trains or provides assistance to athletes as a profession.

As far as physical conditioning is concerned, I believe that most of us would probably love to have the benefit of our own personal physical trainer. This trainer would help — that is, *push* — us toward the goal of a "perfect body."

As I was growing up and participating in athletics, there was no such animal as a personal trainer. The only thing close to that at the time was the coach. Even during my years as a player in the NFL, we didn't have personal trainers during the regular season or in the off-season. In fact, we did our strength and conditioning on our own.

It wasn't until the 1980s that NFL teams started hiring personal trainers, then known as "strength and conditioning coaches" or "strength and conditioning coordinators." Now almost every team in the NFL has two strength and conditioning coaches as well as a speed trainer. Every professional sports team has at least one person that is in charge of the physical fitness program.

In recent years, many pro golfers and tennis players, along with the general public, have hired their own personal trainers to help them with their physical fitness. Tiger Woods was really the one who brought the most national attention to this concept.

As a result of hiring all of these strength and conditioning coaches and personal trainers, professional athletes have seen their performances greatly enhanced on the fields, courts, and courses. Why has this concept of the personal trainer been so effective? I believe that there are several reasons:

1. Personal trainers are trained experts and guides in the areas of physical fitness and nutrition.
2. Because of our fallen human nature, most of us are lazy and won't push ourselves. This includes professional athletes. These personal trainers push athletes to reach their fullest potential. Left on their own, most athletes won't push themselves to the same extent.
3. Personal trainers observe athletes during all phases of their workouts — stretching, lifting, jogging, and running — to see if they are using the proper techniques. If athletes are not using the correct or most effective techniques, personal trainers will make various adjustments to correct the problem so that athletes will get the maximum benefit out of each exercise.
4. Personal trainers are able to check each athlete's daily eating habits to see if he is eating a balanced diet. If he is not receiving the proper nutrition, the personal trainer can make the necessary adjustments. When I was coaching, this became a major problem because so many of our players were single and their diet consisted mostly of fast foods. During the season, this was easier to control because most teams fed their players breakfast and lunch. On the night before a game and on game day, they were fed properly.
5. Personal trainers can monitor, as best they can, athletes' rest and sleeping habits. Sometimes this area is overlooked, but I think it is one of the most important. If an athlete doesn't get his proper rest, it will definitely affect his ability to perform.

When this personal trainer concept was implemented by the NFL in the 1980s, some athletes didn't buy into the concept.

They felt that they could manage their own physical fitness program. Some of my coaching friends who are still in the NFL tell me that there are players on various teams that work out in the off-season on their own and don't participate with the rest of the team under the direction of the strength and conditioning trainer.

Over the years, by and large, players that have participated in these physical fitness programs under the supervision and guidance of personal trainers have tested out with higher scores than the ones that didn't participate. This verifies the value of having a personal trainer guiding you through your physical fitness program, whether you are a professional athlete or not.

The Need for a Personal Trainer in Your Spiritual Workout

When it comes to the spiritual life, it is no different — we tend toward the easiest path, and that path is seldom the most beneficial. A look at the state of Jesus' own disciples in the Gospels makes this abundantly clear.

Prior to the coming of the Holy Spirit at Pentecost, the apostles were not aware of what Jesus was talking about when He taught them. Time and again they were confused by His teachings. The apostles' behavior during Jesus' passion, death, and resurrection was that of a bunch of cowards and scaredy-cats — and the one who seemed to be the most fearful was Peter, the one they called Cephas, which means "Rock." Far from being a solid rock, he was more like a marshmallow. The rest were not much better, spending a lot of time hiding behind locked doors.

But that all changes on the day of Pentecost. When they receive the Holy Spirit, those locked doors are flung open and they fearlessly rush out into the world! They receive an inward power that Jesus had promised them when He said, "You will receive power when the holy Spirit comes upon you" (Acts 1:8).

What happens to that band of cowards once their spiritual Personal Trainer comes into their lives?

1. Their powerlessness suddenly turns into the power to act as Christ acted.
2. They courageously confront the leaders of the people that put Jesus to death.
3. They bear witness to Jesus wherever they go, and they proclaim Him to all.
4. Their transformation amazes all who see or hear it.

In other words, the Holy Spirit that Jesus promised to the apostles is a Personal Trainer who gets results — and gets them fast. Once the Holy Spirit comes into the apostles' lives, their spiritual lives go from zero to 60 in a zip. To put it another way, the Holy Spirit can do for the spiritual life what might take a heavy dose of steroids to do in a physical workout!

St. Luke tells us in the third chapter of Acts that Peter and John cure a crippled beggar. Later on in the same chapter, Peter stands up in Solomon's Portico and boldly accuses those gathered there of failing to accept the "Author of life" and indeed of putting Him to death. In the following chapter, Peter stands before the Sanhedrin and boldly proclaims that Jesus is the Christ, and he invites those who persecuted Jesus to accept Him as the Christ: "There is no salvation through anyone else, nor is there any other name under heaven given to the human race by which we are to be saved" (Acts 4:12).

The reaction of those who witness Peter and John is one of amazement: "Observing the boldness of Peter and John and perceiving them to be uneducated, ordinary men, they were amazed, and they recognized them as the companions of Jesus" (Acts 4:13).

This last verse should make us feel good and instill confidence in us. It proves that God — working through His Holy

Spirit, our Personal Trainer — can take a group of scared, ordinary men and convert them into a bold and courageous group of healers and evangelists. Can you imagine what God can do in your life if you allow Him?

Getting the Holy Spirit as Your Personal Trainer

I am living proof of the miracles that God can work through His Holy Spirit. My spiritual Personal Trainer totally transformed my entire life, and He continues to instruct me each day. Here is my question for you: Why don't you ask God to give you the strength to open up the door to your heart and allow the Holy Spirit, your Personal Trainer, to come into your heart and transform your life?

On the day of Pentecost, Peter told his listeners: "Repent and be baptized, every one of you, in the name of Jesus Christ for the forgiveness of your sins; and you will receive the gift of the holy Spirit" (Acts 2: 38). Repentance is simply admitting that we need God, that we don't know it all, and so we turn to God as though our very life depends upon Him — and it does, whether we are aware of it or not!

You may have been baptized already. But have you died to yourself, and do you live for Christ?

Earthly Spiritual Trainer (Director)

We have just spoken about our heavenly Personal Trainer (or Director), the Holy Spirit. Now I would like to discuss the importance and benefits of acquiring an earthly spiritual director.

It is important for us to have someone in our spiritual life that we can use as our "sounding board," a person that we can turn to on a regular basis to guide us through the many obstacles that we face along the path of our life.

Spiritual direction is concerned with helping a person with his relationship with God. The objective of spiritual direction is to help someone come into a personal relationship with Jesus

Christ and then to monitor how that relationship is lived out in daily life. The direct purpose of spiritual direction is to assist the person in that task.

In his *Spiritual Exercises*, St. Ignatius of Loyola talks about the twofold dynamic movement of Christian spiritual life:

1. The purification "preparing and disposing the soul to rid itself of all inordinate attachments." Thus, spiritual direction should help the person grow in spiritual freedom, freeing him from all that is not God in his life.
2. The concrete surrender to the mystery of God at all times, "after their removal . . . seeing and finding the will of God in the disposition of our life for the salvation of our soul." Thus, spiritual direction should help the person discern the will of God, for ordering his whole life to holiness — union with God.

Choosing the right person as your spiritual director is essential if you are going to receive all the benefits that come from spiritual direction.

The following suggestions are requirements that I used in choosing a spiritual director:

1. The person should be a Catholic in good standing with the Church. This person should also have a fervent prayer life and receive the sacraments regularly.
2. The person should be spiritually mature. In other words, a veteran, not a rookie. This person must be committed to the teaching magisterium of the Church.
3. The person could be priest (which would be great), but that isn't necessary. You may choose a deacon, religious, or layperson that you have confidence in.
4. The person should be a good listener and also someone able to relate well with people.

5. The person should not be a "pushover." You want someone that will tell you the truth and not be a "yes" person.

In my spiritual journey, I have had a priest and a deacon as
my spiritual directors. In fact, I have been blessed because the
deacon that I use just happens to be my sponsor in AA.

TIME OUT!

Let's spend a few moments reflecting on what we've covered
so far:

- How can I enlist the help of the Holy Spirit as my Personal Trainer?
- What steps can I take to invite the Lord into the events of
  my daily life?
- Who is the person I could enlist as an earthly spiritual
  director?
- How can I make all this a priority in my life?

Experiences of Spiritual Direction

During the five years I spent in Chicago, I had Father Peter
Armenio, an Opus Dei priest, as my spiritual director. A friend
of mine, Carmen Sparanza, introduced me to Father Pete.

The first time I formally met Father Pete was when he came
over to my football office at the Chicago Bears practice facility.
My coaching schedule was so crazy during the season that the
only time we could meet was on a Tuesday afternoon. Even
though this was my game-planning day, Father Pete and I were
able to work out a pocket of time.

My first meeting with Father Pete went well, and I knew
that he was the right person for me. He not only made me feel

very comfortable, but he also listened attentively, had a sense of humor, and was orthodox in his approach to the faith.

Father Pete is a little guy in stature, and he really didn't know much about football, but I knew that he loved the Lord and the Catholic Church. I also knew that he took the responsibility of being my spiritual director very seriously.

After our initial meeting, Father Pete and I decided that we would get together every two or three weeks. I was really looking forward to our next visit.

Our next meeting occurred several weeks later in my office, and I finished my session with Father Pete by going to confession. Afterward, as we walked out of my office, we ran into Head Coach Dave Wannstedt in the hallway. So I introduced Dave to Father Pete. Dave asked Father Pete what brought him to Hallas Hall, and Father Pete told him that he was there to give me spiritual direction, along with hearing my confession. Well, Dave immediately asked Father Pete if he would hear his confession, which, of course, Father Pete agreed to do.

To make a long story short, Father Pete started visiting every three weeks, not only to see me but also to see Coach Wannstedt and some of the other coaches. Eventually, Father Pete started giving spiritual direction to several of our Protestant coaches. Finally, some of the players asked him if he could meet with them, too. This continued for the next several years, until I left the Bears in 1997 to take a job with the New Orleans Saints.

Even though I was gone, Father Pete had already established some powerful spiritual relationships, and he remained the spiritual director for Coach Wannstedt and many of the coaches and players. What is even more amazing, when Coach Wannstedt left the Bears — becoming the head coach of the Miami Dolphins — Father Pete established a spiritual connection with the new head coach, Dick Juron, and some of his assistant coaches. The Holy Spirit can make things happen in the most unlikely places.

The combination of our spiritual Personal Trainer (the Holy Spirit) and our earthly spiritual director makes for a great "one-two punch." Ask the Holy Spirit to direct you to the person that would be the best one for you to use as your spiritual director.

Final Advice

Cardinal Joseph Mercier was once asked what he thought was the key to growing closer to God. His answer is the perfect advice for anyone who wants to employ the Holy Spirit as his Personal Trainer in this spiritual workout:

QUOTE

Every day, for five minutes restrain your imagination; close your eyes, as it were, and your ears, to all earthly impressions so as to be able to withdraw into the sanctuary of your baptized soul, the Temple of God within. Then address the Holy Spirit in words like this:

> O Holy Spirit, Beloved of my soul, I adore you.
> Enlighten, strengthen, guide, comfort, and console me.
> Tell me what I ought to do and command me to do it.
> I promise to be submissive in everything that you permit to happen to me,
> only show me what is your will
> [and give me the grace to do it].

Cardinal Mercier promised, "If you do this, you will spend your life in contentment and peace. You will have abundant consolation even amidst troubles, for you will receive grace in proportion to your burdens, until the day when you will reach heaven weighted with precious merits."

ACTION PLAN

Things to Do

- Invoke the aid of your Personal Trainer, the Holy Spirit.
- Seek out an earthly spiritual director.

Scripture: Matthew 6:33
"Seek first the kingdom [of God]."

Scout the Enemies of Your Spiritual Life

Scouting Reports in the National Football League

During the NFL season, Mondays begin with the preparation of a scouting report on a team's next opponent. This report is compiled over a two-day time period and is presented to the players on Wednesday.

A scouting report is broken down to cover the following areas: personnel, offense, defense, special teams, and finally a game plan. Here is a brief outline of what happens with the first three — personnel, offense, and defense:

Personnel: A report is compiled on each player of the opposing team beginning with each individual's height and weight, his background, and his strengths and weaknesses (such as speed, quickness, and physical strength). There is also an investigation to see if a player has suffered any injuries. The focus is placed on the starters of the opposing team.

The opponent's offense and defense are studied. Each individual position's coach studies previous game tapes, usually paying special attention to the last three games to help with the evaluation. After the individual coaches watch these tapes, they come together as offensive and defensive staffs and then watch more game tapes together, trying to narrow down the opponent's tendencies.

Offense: Offensive coaches are looking at several key things that make the opponent's defense either effective or vulnerable:

1. What are their key fronts and coverages?
2. Are they aggressive or passive?

3. Do they like to gamble, using a lot of blitzes, or do they play conservatively?
4. What types of personnel groups do they use on long-yardage situations?
5. Are they more effective against the run or the pass?
6. What do they do on goal-line and short-yardage situations?

Defense: Defensive coaches are looking for the following in evaluating the opponent's offense:

1. What style of offense do they run (for example, West Coast)?
2. What are their formations and motions?
3. Are they wide open or conservative?
4. Do they have big-play capacity?
5. Are they vulnerable to the blitz?
6. What personnel groups do they use on third downs?
7. Are they run- or pass-oriented, or are they balanced?
8. What do they do in goal-line and short-yardage situations?

These are just some of the areas that are involved in the scouting report that eventually leads to the final game plan that is used on Sunday. Once the coaches have completed the scouting report and the game plan, it is presented to the players on Wednesday morning.

One particular Wednesday morning when I was the offensive co-coordinator of the New Orleans Saints, I walked down to the meeting room, where I was going to present a clever game plan that our coaching staff had worked out for that week's game. Since it was a departure from our normal tendencies, I remember thinking as I approached the meeting room, "I don't feel very comfortable with this plan."

About halfway through my presentation, I could see that many of the players were getting a glazed-over look in their eyes and weren't picking up the game plan that I was presenting to them. I knew they were thinking, "Now, what in the hell are these coaches trying to do?"

After the morning meetings, I called the other coaches into my office and told them that we were throwing out all that new crap we had put in and just stick with the basics. You see, we had devised this elaborate scheme that we thought would trick our opponent, but unfortunately all it did was confuse our own players. A game plan is good only if it is understood by those who have to put it into action, and knowing our "enemy's" strengths and weaknesses can help only if we are fully aware of our own.

Once an NFL scouting report and game plan are presented on Wednesday morning to the players, the team then goes out onto the field for the next three days and practices the game plan. Certain adjustments are made during this practice period, taking into account how the coaches judge the effectiveness and ability of the team's players to carry it out.

A Spiritual Scouting Report

As far as our spiritual life is concerned, we can also devise a scouting report that is similar to the one that is used in the NFL. Every NFL team must come up with a new scouting report and game plan every week of the season. In the spiritual arena, I think we need to prepare only one overall scouting report and game plan for life. But we will still need to revise it periodically when our life's circumstances change.

The content of a spiritual scouting report and the one used in the NFL will be somewhat similar, but the spiritual game plan itself will be quite different from the NFL's.

The spiritual scouting report must consist of the following areas: personnel, offense, and defense. Lastly, there is the game plan.

A Look at Personnel: The Man in the Mirror

An NFL scouting report deals with the opposing team's personnel. In a spiritual scouting report, the personnel that we will study are ourselves. Basically, we will evaluate our strengths and weaknesses, successes and failures.

What really helped me when I was trying to complete this section on self-evaluation were things that I learned from two of the steps in the twelve-step AA program. Both of these steps can be found in the book *Alcoholics Anonymous* — sometimes referred to as the "Big Book" — in the fifth chapter titled "How It works."

The first step that helped me was Step Four: "Made a searching and fearless moral inventory of ourselves."

This inventory took me quite a long time to complete — over a year, in fact. My AA sponsor advised me to take my time doing this and not to get uptight, feeling that I had to accomplish it by such and such a date. He said that it was more important to dig down deep inside and to bring everything out — to really be fearless in taking a good hard look at the "man in the mirror." This was not easy for me to do, because I was dealing with a lot of hurt and guilt. That's why it took me so long.

I should mention another very helpful hint that my sponsor told me. He said, "Don't just focus on the negative things, but be sure to include the positive things about yourself, too!"

The fact that I am a Catholic helped me out dramatically with the "how-to" part of this Fourth Step. Basically, this AA step is nothing more than a thorough examination of conscience, which I had learned years earlier when I was preparing for my first confession. It is something we Catholics are supposed to do each time we go to confession.

Many of us carry around an image of ourselves that is based more on how we think others view us, rather than what we truly are. Thomas Merton called this image the "false self," and he contrasted it with the "true self," which is the person God created us to be. This true self will emerge when we put God first in our lives and seek to please Him. The false self is an illusion; it isn't who we are, and it leads to all kinds of problems for the person who confuses his identity with it.

Take a good, long, hard look at yourself. What are your talents? What do you like to do? What do you do because you think it will win you acceptance from others? How true are you to the commitments you have made in your life? Are you a good husband to your wife? Are you a good father to your children? Are you a good son to your parents? What are your weaknesses?

Now that you know your weaknesses and your commitments in life, what occasions of sin should you avoid?

The second step that helped me was Step Five:

"Admitted to God, to ourselves, and to another human being the exact nature of our wrongs."

This step wasn't quite as difficult as the Fourth Step. I'll explain why.

I had made plans to go on a three-day silent retreat when I was about finished with the Fourth Step inventory. I was going to put the finishing touches on this step, which I did, but much to my surprise I found myself being urged inwardly (by my Personal Trainer, the Holy Spirit) to make an appointment with one of the priests on staff to hear my confession (part of my fulfillment of the Fifth Step). This Fifth Step is nothing more than celebrating the Sacrament of Reconciliation — confession — which I did. I was able to complete the Fourth and Fifth Steps and make a general confession at the same time so that I could get back into the state of God's grace.

I encourage you to do these steps: to take stock of your life and to make a general confession. This is another opportunity to enlist the help of your Personal Trainer. Ask Him not only to reveal to you your strengths and weaknesses but also to shed light into the areas of your life where you need to repent of your sins. Ask Him for His help and guidance in repairing the damage that your sins have inflicted on you and others (or ask God to bring healing) and for the grace for you to know sorrow for your sins. Finally, ask the Holy Spirit for the grace to lead you to a good confessor who will help you make a good confession.

NFL coaches study their opponent's offense and defense, whereas in our spiritual scouting report we must study *our* offensive and defensive activities or actions as they apply to the way we live our lives.

Our Offense

Who's calling our plays? What is motivating us? What is in the end zone — what is the goal of our life?

In order for us to have an effective spiritual scouting report, we must reflect back over many years to determine exactly what our priorities in life have been, as they pertain to the physical, intellectual, and spiritual aspects of our life. In other words, what really matters to us? What are our priorities in life?

➥ Is It to Leave Behind a Great Body?

Each year we Americans spend an incredible amount of money trying to get our physical bodies into shape by frequenting health clubs, beauty salons, and tanning booths, as well as experimenting with nutritional supplements, diet programs, and pills. The health-and-beauty industry is huge, with annual revenues in the billions of dollars.

Many of us spend an excessive amount of time, money, and effort to make our bodies beautiful. In fact, if we had the talent and worked hard enough, we could even possibly win a Mr. America weightlifting contest, or have an opportunity to become a movie star, or even play in the NFL.

While there is nothing wrong with caring about our bodies and our physical looks, I think we have become almost obsessed with it. At the fitness club that I belong to, they tell me that people are standing in line at 5:30 a.m. for the doors to open so that they can begin their spinning classes.

Thousand upon thousands of people are having surgery for face-lifts, nose jobs, hair replacements, and liposuction — and all of this for one reason: to make us look younger and better-looking.

Yet, is this a worthy priority in life, or is it an escape from reality? One thing is certain, and it's a scientifically proven fact: Our physical body will let us down one day, and *we will die*. The words that we hear when ashes are placed on our foreheads on Ash Wednesday clearly illustrate this point: "Remember, you are dust, and to dust you will return."

ꜱ Is It to Be the Smartest Guy on the Block?

For some, it is their intellectual life. The knowledge we obtain through education prepares us for our vocation in life. Currently, we begin the education process at a very young age and extend it beyond the ordinary four-year college program. Many are encouraged to obtain advanced degrees.

In today's business world, companies are offering programs with specialized training, especially in the area of computer technology. With the rapid advancement of this technology, we are now capable of educating and training people more effectively and quickly. The various discoveries and accomplishments in the fields of science and medicine are amazing and often mind-boggling.

Education provides the opportunities to become almost anything imaginable. People from very humble backgrounds can become doctors, lawyers, and engineers. One can achieve the highest awards or offices, such as the Nobel Peace Prize, the Pulitzer Prize, or perhaps even being elected president of the United States.

But no matter how many academic degrees, awards, or public offices a person obtains, one thing is absolutely certain: All of this comes to an abrupt end upon death. So, if competing to have the most degrees and recognition is what drives you, then you're driving down a dead-end road!

⌇ Is It Your Spiritual Life?

On the other hand, the spiritual aspect of our life deals with the interior portion — the heart and soul — of who we are as human beings. There is a huge difference between the physical and intellectual aspects and the spiritual. As mentioned earlier, the physical and intellectual end at death, whereas the spiritual lasts forever. In His discourse at the Last Supper, Jesus says this:

QUOTE

"In my Father's house there are many dwelling places. If there were not, would I have told you that I am going to prepare a place for you? And if I go and prepare a place for you, I will come back again and take you to myself, so that where I am you also may be."

JOHN 14:2-3

TIME OUT!

Find a quiet place where you can spend some time reflecting on these two questions:

- How much time each day do I spend on the physical and intellectual parts of my life, which I know for certain will end?

- How much time each day do I spend on my spiritual life, which Jesus has assured me will last forever?

If you are like most men in this world, and if you answer these questions truthfully, you probably spend a disproportionately greater amount of time on the physical and intellectual aspects of your life as compared to the amount of time you spend on the spiritual.

Our Defense

It really doesn't matter which priority we are living for right now, even if it is one of the two that will end at death. There are always obstacles blocking the way to our goals. In fact, it is clear that if you are living for the physical or the intellectual, then death is the ultimate obstacle, one that you cannot overcome without help. Thankfully, God has sent His Son to save us!

In order to develop a game plan for life, we need to look at what keeps us from being more spiritual. What are the obstacles we are likely to encounter in our pursuit to follow Jesus Christ in our lives?

Reflecting on Our Blocking Schemes

 TIME OUT!

Now it's time to do some heavy lifting. In order to get the most out of this exercise, ask your Personal Trainer, the Holy Spirit, to shed some light on how you should answer the following questions:
- What keeps me from focusing on the most important part of my life?
- What can I do to change this pattern in my life?

The answers to these questions are important, if we are to develop a personal game plan that will take into account our unique situation in life. Following the plan laid out in the rest of this book requires complete honesty at this level. We have to find a way to make "what really matters" — our relationship with God — the top priority in our life and to come up with a plan that will overcome all obstacles that keep us from reaching that goal.

Our Game Plan

You are probably asking yourself right now, "How much time should I be devoting to my spiritual life?" The answer is: All of it. This doesn't mean that you have to spend special "alone time" with God at every moment, but it does mean that God and His will for you have to always be on your mind and in your heart. In the same way that any physical program requires a total commitment of how we spend all of our time, so does a spiritual workout. St. Paul counsels us, "Pray without ceasing" (1 Thessalonians 5:17). Every moment of the day requires a spiritual alertness. As St. Peter says: "Be sober and vigilant. Your opponent the devil is prowling around like a roaring lion looking for [someone] to devour" (1 Peter 5:8).

We must remember that we were created in God's image and likeness, and that we owe everything to God our Creator. The only thing that God wants from us is our love. The Lord spoke these words to Moses:

QUOTE

"Hear, O Israel! The LORD is our God, the LORD alone! Therefore, you shall love the LORD, your God, with all your heart, and with all your soul, and with all your strength."

DEUTERONOMY 6:4-5

And Jesus gave this reply to a scribe who had asked him, "Which is the first of all the commandments?" (Mark 12:28):

QUOTE

"Hear, O Israel! The Lord our God is Lord alone! You shall love the Lord your God with all your heart, with all your soul, with all your mind, and with all your strength."

MARK 12:29-30

St. Ignatius of Loyola, in "First Principle and Foundation" of his *Spiritual Exercises* — or today what we might call a mission statement — wrote about the solid foundation that we should build our spiritual lives on:

QUOTE

Man is created to praise, reverence, and serve God our Lord, and by this means to save his soul.

And the other things on the face of the earth are created for man that they may help him in prosecuting the end for which he is created.

From this it follows that man is to use them as much as they help him on to his end, and ought to rid himself of them so far as they hinder him as to it.

FROM *THE SPIRITUAL EXERCISES: A LITERAL TRANSLATION AND A CONTEMPORARY READING* (ST. LOUIS, INSTITUTE OF JESUIT SOURCES, 1978)

God made us for a purpose: to serve Him here on earth and then to live forever with Him in Paradise. God is like the United Way. All He wants us to do is give Him His fair share. But unlike the United Way, God's fair share is our very lives.

Every person, regardless of where he or she stands spiritually, needs to develop an ongoing spiritual relationship with God. The Gospel reminds us that Jesus Christ is "the way and the truth and the life" (John 14:6) and calls us to live our lives in a deeper, spiritual way. St. Augustine tells us that "our hearts will never rest until they rest with Thee."

QUOTE

We are not discouraged; rather, although our outer self is wasting away, our inner self is being renewed day by day.
2 CORINTHIANS 4:16

These words of St. Paul sum up one of the paradoxes of the Christian life: Whereas the outer person, in the perishable body, is wasting away due to tribulation and affliction, the inner person, in the life of the soul, is growing and being renewed day by day, until the point comes when it reaches its full growth in heaven.

The NFL team we were speaking of earlier in this chapter has now completed all the necessary details leading up to game day on Sunday. The scouting report has been presented, the game plan has been implemented, practice time is over, and now it's "showtime."

So what is our game plan? It is laid out in the rest of this book, and it involves enlisting our Personal Trainer, knowing ourselves, stretching out in prayer, running toward God, powerlifting, and getting good nutrition and proper rest. We've looked at the first two, and we'll deal with the others in detail in the remaining chapters of this book.

Encouragement

Sometimes our best-laid plans go awry. I can remember a few games in my career as a player and as a coach when, after all the preparation, we thought we had the perfect game plan, but then on Sunday we found ourselves trailing by two touchdowns before the national anthem had been sung. A week's worth of work — and in a matter of three hours, it was all for naught.

There will always be a winner and a loser, and the following week another winner and loser. And finally, at the end of the season, a Super Bowl champion.

(Oh yeah, what about the Super Bowl loser? The winner receives the Lombardi Trophy. The only good thing that comes out of losing the Super Bowl is that you have an opportunity to come back and compete for the Super Bowl the next year.)

Now your spiritual scouting report has been completed. It's time to implement our game plan, "The Spiritual Fitness Workout," that will prepare us for our spiritual super bowl. The competition in this super bowl pits the world, the flesh, and the devil against us and our Personal Trainer, the Holy Spirit.

QUOTE

For those who live according to the flesh are concerned with the things of the flesh, but those who live according to the spirit with the things of the spirit. The concern of the flesh is death, but the concern of the spirit is life and peace. . . . [T]hose who are in the flesh cannot please God.

ROMANS 8:5-6, 8

The kickoff is about to begin. The length of this game is not three hours like an NFL game but instead lasts a lifetime. The only one who knows when our game will end is God. So we must be prepared.

The winner has a reward much greater than the Lombardi Trophy. The winner receives the reward of eternal happiness with the Father. Oh yeah, what about the loser? For him there is no tomorrow. There is no opportunity to come back and play again. The loser's soul remains in hell for all eternity.

I am sorry to scare you like this, but we are in a battle of spiritual warfare, and the stakes are for all eternity and not just for another trophy or bragging rights for having won a game. And it is a team effort. So, men, we must strive to get ourselves into spiritual fitness so that we can lead our families, relatives, and friends to a victory that is beyond any earthly victory.

ACTION PLAN

Things to Do

- Spend some time over the next few weeks and take an inventory of your life.
- Rearrange the priorities to reflect:
    God — First
    Family — Second
    Job, etc. — Third, etc.

Scripture: Matthew 22:37-39

"You shall love the Lord, your God, with all your heart, with all your soul, and with all your mind. This is the greatest and the first commandment. The second is like it: You shall love your neighbor as yourself."

STEP THREE

Stretch Out in Prayer

The Need for Stretching

Athletes know that if they don't prepare themselves with a little stretching before beginning a rigorous workout, they risk tearing muscles. The same is true for a spiritual workout. Before we do the heavy lifting and running, we need to do some "warm-up" exercises.

Spiritual stretching requires the developing of a habit of prayer. Prayer is the key to beginning and sustaining a successful spiritual workout. If you don't stretch out spiritually in prayer, then you won't grow inwardly, and eventually your life will become empty. But on the other hand, if you establish a spiritual fitness program that focuses on stretching out daily in prayer as its core, you will notice that your spiritual life will be enhanced by the building up of the "muscles" of your heart, strengthening them in the virtues of faith, hope, and charity.

 QUOTE

A spiritual writer, Father Ignacio Larranaga, has pointed out the strange law of prayer, "The more one prays, the more one wants to pray," and vice versa, "The less one prays, the less one wants to pray." There is a correlation between action and desire. So the important thing right up front with prayer is to do it, and the desire to do it will follow.

In my own life, it took me quite some time before I began to realize how important prayer was to my spiritual stability.

After years of trying to accomplish things on my own, I came to the conclusion that I needed to turn to God, through prayer, for all my needs.

What Is Prayer?

Prayer is essentially an intimate conversation with God in which the soul seeks His presence so that it may speak with Him in a friendly and affectionate way.

Prayer is not an act of attempting to manipulate God but instead a means of giving God thanks and praise, calling upon Him for one's daily needs and the care of others, and asking that His will be done and that His kingdom come.

In the *Pocket Catholic Dictionary*, by Father John Hardon, prayer is defined as "the voluntary response to the awareness of God's presence." Father Hardon explains, "The response may be an acknowledgement of God's greatness and of a person's total dependence on Him (adoration) or gratitude for His benefits to oneself and others (thanksgiving) or sorrow for sins committed and begging for mercy (expiation) or asking for graces needed (petitions) or affections for God, who is all good (love)."

The *Catechism of the Catholic Church* teaches, " 'Prayer is the raising of one's mind and heart to God or the requesting of good things from God.' " It also says: "*Humility* is the foundation of prayer. Only when we humbly acknowledge that 'we do not know how to pray as we ought,' are we ready to receive freely the gift of prayer" (no. 2559).

Preparation

To have a more comprehensive understanding of the meaning of prayer, read Part Four of the *Catechism*, which deals explicitly with the subject of prayer. This section of the *Catechism* thoroughly explains what prayer is, why we should pray, what Scripture says about prayer, and the Church's position on prayer. Most importantly, it reveals what Jesus thought of prayer, how He prayed, how He taught His disciples to pray, and how He hears our prayers.

Reflecting on Our Prayer Life

TIME OUT!

Spend a few minutes answering the following questions about your prayer life:

- How often do I pray?
- How do I pray?
- Do I pray as though I'm talking to someone, or do I just mutter my prayers, with no sense that they are going anywhere?
- Do I pray with faith that God hears my prayers and can act decisively in my life and in the lives of others?

Even if your prayer life has been less than stellar, there is hope. By reading the section in the *Catechism* on prayer, you will receive the necessary encouragement and guidance to commit to some form of prayer in your life. It will also point out how all of the great leaders of the Church have depended on prayer to guide them through their lives.

The Example of the Head Coach

The Gospels clearly show the importance of prayer in the life and ministry of Jesus Christ, our Head Coach. On numerous occasions in Scripture, we find Jesus (our Head Coach) either going out to various places to pray alone or inviting His apostles (the Coaching Staff) to join Him so that He can teach them how to pray.

QUOTE

Jesus prays *before* the decisive moments of his mission; before his Father's witness to him during his baptism and Transfiguration, and before his own fulfillment of the Father's plan of love by his Passion (cf. Lk 3:21; 9:28; 22:41-44). He also prays before the decisive moments involving the mission of his apostles: at his election and call of the Twelve, before Peter's confession of him as "the Christ of God," and again that the faith of the chief of the Apostles may not fail when tempted (cf. Lk 6:12; 9:18-20; 22:32).

CATECHISM OF THE CATHOLIC CHURCH, NO. 2600

As a former NFL coach, I was helped and encouraged in my prayer life by the example of Jesus' (our Head Coach's) commitment to prayer. It is especially interesting to note that Jesus prayed not only in critical times, but He also stretched out in prayer daily and taught others to do the same.

St. Luke tells us that "[Jesus] was praying in a certain place, and when he had finished, one of his disciples said to him, 'Lord, teach us to pray just as John taught his disciples.' He said to them, 'When you pray, say: / Father, hallowed be your name, / your kingdom come. / Give us each day our daily bread / and forgive us our sins / for we ourselves forgive everyone in debt to us, / and do not subject us to the final test' " (Luke 11:1-4).

These words that Jesus spoke to His apostles should encourage those who want to pray but who don't know how to begin. Imitate the apostles and ask your Personal Trainer, the Holy Spirit, to teach you how to pray. Then follow the instructions in the *Catechism* on prayer, and you will be able to start praying.

Sometime ago, I had an experience that convinced me to abandon my "hit and miss" approach to prayer and commit to stretch out in prayer on a daily basis. I was praying one day, and all of a sudden I said to myself: "If Jesus thought that much about prayer, that He prayed that often, then why shouldn't I be praying each and every day?"

The Examples of Others

Traveling further through the Scriptures, we begin to notice what an important role prayer played in people's lives. The Scriptures indicate to us that prayer effectively changed the lives of the prophets and disciples.

As we study the history of the Church and probe the lives of many of the saints and Fathers of the Church, we begin to see how each one established his or her own form of prayer life. The spectrum ranges from contemplative prayer all the way to the very emotional charismatic prayer style.

Our modern-day Church has many fine examples of God's people who are known for their fervent prayer life. One of the greatest witnesses has been Pope John Paul II. Because of his commitment to daily prayer, I believe that the Holy Spirit has supplied him with the graces and power necessary to accomplish all the things he has set out to do, even in times of failing health and old age.

Another great example is Blessed Mother Teresa of Calcutta. The order of nuns she founded, the Missionaries of Charity, remain devoted to a rigid daily prayer life that Mother Teresa held as an absolute necessity. The powerful ministry that she established continues to flourish long after her death because of her sisters' dedication to daily prayer.

On a more personal basis, there have been two people in my life whose lives of prayer have been tremendous examples to me. Through her fervent and simple prayer life, my grandmother Babka Abramowicz, a Polish immigrant, has had a significant impact on my own prayer life. Her motto was "Idle hands create idle minds" — that's why she always had a rosary in her hand. She lived until the ripe old age of 98, still maintaining that simple prayer life, one that not only made a great difference in the way she lived her own life but also served as an inspiration to all who knew her.

The other person who has had a dramatic and lasting influence on my prayer life is my father, Paper Abramowicz. Even though our family faced some difficult times when I was growing up, I always remember Dad either going to Mass, praying the Rosary, or reciting a novena. Today, at age 84, he is a daily communicant. He also sets aside special time for prayer each morning and visits the adoration chapel each afternoon at two o'clock. Then, just as faithfully, he goes to the American Legion or the Polish Athletic Club and meets my father-in-law, Pepper DiPrinizo, for a few beers and to aggravate all the other patrons!

You've probably noticed my father's and father-in-law's names, Paper and Pepper. Most people use nicknames in my hometown, rather than their real names. One time I ran into a guy at the airport, and he proceeded to tell me that he met a friend of mine, John Taylor. I just couldn't put a face to the name until the person told me that he thought John said that I might remember him by the name "Goose." And, of course, I remembered immediately — "Goose" Taylor — one of my closest childhood friends.

Who Are the Great Pray-ers I Know?

TIME OUT!

Hopefully, these examples of people show the importance and effectiveness of prayer. Spend a few moments thinking about the following questions:

• Who are the people I have known as great pray-ers?

- What enabled them to stay committed to prayer?
- Who are the people I would seek out to pray for me in a difficult situation?
- Could these people help me improve or establish my prayer life?

Hopefully the examples of these people will encourage you enough to begin this spiritual workout program sooner, rather than later.

Four Steps to "Stretching Out" in Prayer

Talking about prayer is one thing; making it a part of your life requires hard work. I have come up with four steps to do just that, and I'd like to share them with you.

⮑ First: Make the Commitment to Pray

Above all else, you must make a commitment to pray daily. When you commit yourself to praying, you are consciously dedicating your time and effort to this undertaking. This means that you are very serious about prayer, and that you acknowledge the need for prayer in your life. This commitment will help you combat the many distractions that you can expect to face, such as being too tired, too busy, not in the mood, just to name a few. Whenever people commit themselves to do something, it becomes more difficult for them to back off their obligation when things become very challenging.

Let me give you a personal example showing why a commitment is so necessary. When I first started praying on a consistent basis many years ago, everything moved along quite nicely for several months. I had experienced God's presence during my prayer time on numerous occasions and felt a sense of peace. But suddenly one day, for the first time, I experienced and felt nothing during prayer.

This period of dryness continued for several weeks, and it concerned me enough that I turned to a priest-friend (my spiritual director) for advice. I felt quite relieved when he informed me that "dryness in prayer" occurs often in people's prayer life, and that I just needed to persevere and pray my way through it. He also mentioned something that has been very helpful to me over the years: A successful prayer life is not based on our feelings or our emotions. He went on to say that a true prayer warrior is one that consistently prays no matter what the circumstances are in life. He said that we should pray in good times and in bad, through trials and tribulations, and in sickness and in health.

I realized that had I not made a personal commitment to daily prayer, I probably would have become discouraged during that dry spell and abandoned my prayer time.

⇔ Second: Take the Time to Pray

Once you have decided to commit yourself to praying, the next factor to consider is the amount of time you will spend stretching out in prayer.

The old adage "time is of the essence" is apropos. Our time is a very precious commodity, and it should be utilized properly. If you think about it, we really have no control over the amount of time we will spend on this earth. Some people may live to the ripe old age of 98, like my Babka, and others may pass away at a very young age. Nobody really knows. Only one has that information, and God isn't giving it out!

This reminds me of something that happened many years ago. I was speaking at a high school, and the fire alarm went off. Everyone evacuated the building orderly and quickly. At the time, no one knew for certain whether the alarm was for real or not. Apparently, the school had received a bomb threat, and the bomb squad was called in to investigate. Thank goodness it was a false alarm.

When we reentered the building, the Lord spoke to me and advised me to ask the students the following question: "If that had been a real bomb and if it had gone off with all of us in the building, would you have been prepared to meet your maker?"

TIME OUT!

If you had been one of those students, what would your answer have been?

Surveys before September 11, 2001, seem to indicate that the number of people who prayed on a regular basis was on the decline. Several reasons were given, but one of the most often-used excuses was that people just couldn't find enough time during the day to fit it in. Isn't it amazing how we can't find time to pray during the day, but we have plenty of time to devote to many of our other interests. For instance, statistics show that the average American woman spends 33 hours a week watching television. I would like to see the stats on the hours men spend watching sports. I also think it would be interesting to find out how much time we spend on cell phones and computers, or listening to music and sports talk shows, or going to movies and bars. It seems that a lot more time is spent on our temporal wants than on our spiritual needs.

Time will escape us if we do not manage it wisely. Whenever I speak to people about their physical workout programs, I advise them to schedule it for a specific time and day. If you do not schedule a time to work out, you'll find yourself missing workouts for one reason or another. The next thing you know, you are not working out at all.

The same thing holds true for prayer. My recommendation is that you make an "appointment" with Jesus and put it on your daily schedule. If you do not force yourself to schedule prayer at a specific time, you will start missing your appointments sporadically, and then you will become discouraged and eventually may even get totally away from praying.

I began my prayer life with much enthusiasm, but I did not start it in an organized manner. Basically, I began praying on certain days, at certain times, with no real rhyme or reason. After many months using this hit-or-miss approach, I found myself becoming very frustrated and losing my enthusiasm for prayer. I finally realized that to solve this recurring problem, it was necessary to find and set aside a specific prayer time that fitted into my daily schedule.

After much thinking and praying about this situation, I came to the conclusion that prayer was at the top of my priority list; and if that was the case, then I should begin each morning by stretching out in prayer. So I began with 15 minutes daily. As I became comfortable with that amount of time, I began to increase it in five-minute intervals until I reached 45 minutes. Presently, I am spending 45 minutes praying each weekday morning, and on the weekends my wife and I pray together for approximately 90 minutes. My wife also prays for 45 minutes during the weekday.

This routine does get disrupted from time to time, and I adjust my schedule. For example, I may have an early morning meeting or I may be traveling and will find it necessary to fit prayer time elsewhere in my schedule. However, I make every effort to include prayer time each day.

I must be perfectly honest with you. Whenever I try praying at night, more often than not I fall asleep in my easy chair. The books or beads land in my lap, my glasses fall off my nose, and my head begins to bob. As always, the snoring alerts my wife, and she sweetly asks me when I finally open my eyes, as I'm trying to get the kink out of my neck and the slobber off my chin: "Papa, how was your prayer time?" Of course, I never admit that I've nodded off, and I resume my prayers as if nothing ever happened.

Maybe you can start out like I did, with a commitment of 15 minutes a day. If you make prayer a high priority in your life, you will be able to find 15 minutes of time to be with Our Lord in prayer.

Remember that all of us are unique, and that what might work for one person might not work for another. It so happens that my favorite prayer time is in the morning. Your favorite time might be in the middle of the day or maybe in the late evening, if you work all day. What is most important is to (1) determine the amount of time you want to spend, (2) decide when you want to spend it, and (3) write it on your calendar — and then just go for it!

At first, you may experience some difficulty trying to adjust your schedule. But once you get yourself organized, you will thoroughly enjoy stretching out in prayer. In fact, you will look forward to this time each day — and if for some reason you happen to miss, you will experience a sense of emptiness during the day.

Finally, all of us must be aware of the need to overcome the various temptations and distractions that we face in trying to pray. The Gospels remind us that after Jesus' baptism and time of prayer, He was tempted by Satan in the desert. The same thing happens to us. Why? Because even Satan knows that prayer can totally transform a person's life, and the devil wants to prevent that from happening at all cost.

⇨ Third: Find a Place to Pray

Once the commitments to pray and to set aside a time to pray have been established, the next step is to find a place to pray. The main consideration is that it be a quiet or silent place. Ideally, there should be no background noise from radios, televisions, telephones, fax machines, or any other outside disturbances.

Quiet is of the utmost importance because it provides the proper environment for us to listen to God. Our world is cluttered with so much noise. Everywhere we turn, people are wearing headsets, music is blaring from cars, televisions are on constantly, and cell phones are ringing — even in church. It is impossible for us to hear God communicating with us under these conditions.

Every so often, I go on a retreat at Manresa, a Jesuit facility on the banks of the Mississippi River. This is a place of absolute tranquility. The only rule for this four-day retreat is that everyone must observe complete silence. If you break the silence, they ask you to go home. On the front of their retreat manual, there is a prayer that was written by a retreatant:

> The house of silence and sacred sod, where nobody speaks to anybody, and everybody speaks to God.

The place that you choose should be somewhere that you feel comfortable and relaxed. The following are some suggestions:

- Sit in your favorite chair.
- Sit or kneel on the floor, possibly in a secluded room.
- Find a spot in the backyard — and if you happen to have a fountain, that makes it even better.
- Sit on a swing or chair on the back porch.

Some of you may be blessed enough to have a house on a lake or one tucked away in the woods. This makes it easier to find a quiet and serene place to pray.

Some people arrive at work early, close the door to their office, and spend time in prayer. For those of you who travel quite extensively, find a section of the airport that will provide you with some quiet time for prayer. If much of your time is consumed traveling in a car, consider praying the Rosary, listening to "chants" from monasteries, or reflecting on audiotapes of the Scriptures, homilies, or Catholic teachings.

There are many locations indoors or out that lend themselves to a peaceful prayer environment.

QUOTES

The Scriptures point out to us that Jesus enjoyed going off to quiet places for prayer, with mountains as favorite spots:

He went up on the mountain by himself to pray. When it was evening he was there alone.

MATTHEW 14:23

Rising very early before dawn, he left and went off to a deserted place, where he prayed.

MARK 1:35

In those days he departed to the mountain to pray, and he spent the night in payer to God.

LUKE 6:12

In addition, Moses, the lawgiver, was known for going to the mountaintop for prayer time with God. The Lord spoke to Moses:

"Get ready for tomorrow morning, when you are to go up Mount Sinai and there present yourself to me on the top of the mountain. . . ." Moses at once bowed down to the ground in worship.

EXODUS 34:2, 8

So where is your mountaintop place? I recommend that you find a place that feels comfortable to you and go with it. My favorite chair that sits in the corner of our great room is my mountaintop place.

⮂ Fourth: Develop a Format of Prayer

To have an effective and organized prayer time, I feel it is necessary to have a basic format to follow. Participants in a physical workout program follow a format schedule. The same thing holds true with a prayer schedule.

I would like to share with you a basic format that I have used, which may be helpful to you in organizing your prayer time.

Praise and Thanksgiving

I always start my stretching out in prayer by allotting several minutes to praising and thanking God for all of His blessings. I praise Him for being my God and my Creator, and I recognize that without Him in my life I am nothing.

QUOTE

St. Paul writes that there is "one God, the Father, / from whom all things are and for whom we exist" (1 Corinthians 8:6).

I thoroughly enjoy reading the Psalms because their verses are filled with songs of praise and worship. For example, in Psalm 138:1-3, we pray: "I thank you, LORD, with all my heart; / before the gods to you I sing. / I bow low toward your holy temple; / I praise your name for your fidelity and love. / For you have exalted over all / your name and your promise."

A friend of mine recommended that during my praise time, on occasion, I should lift my hands to acknowledge my awe of God. At first, this was not easy to do — in fact, it was as if I were trying to lift a ton of bricks. Finally, I decided to raise my hands in honor of my God. I believe that men have a more difficult time than women in doing this because of our macho self-image. It is a sign of weakness to some men. To me, it has been a relief, because it helps me to remain humble before the Lord. I notice that thousands of us attending sporting events and concerts have no problem raising our hands to cheer for these celebrities, but we can't raise our hands to God. That doesn't make any sense.

I also like to give thanks to God for His many blessings, such as: "I thank You, God, for my faith. I thank You for my family, especially for our recently born grandson, Dillon. I thank You for my job, my health, and the very breath that I take."

I also thank Him for the trials, tribulations, and sufferings that He permits in my life and my family. All that I ask of Him is the strength and the courage to deal with these situations whenever they occur.

Another absolutely wonderful and simple way to praise and thank the Lord is by the invocation of the holy name of Jesus. When the holy name is repeated often by a humbly attentive heart, it is not otherwise lost by heaping up empty phrases. The total focus of the prayer is simply on that one word: Jesus. I utilize this form of prayer whenever my mind drifts off during my prayer time. This simple prayer is the most effective way to counteract a wandering mind.

Spiritual Reading
Part of my prayer time is devoted to reading spiritual material and then reflecting on how I can apply what I have read to my own life. The reading of the Scriptures, especially the Gospels, will supply you with a wealth of material for contemplation.

I also recommend *Magnificat*, a wonderful monthly magazine/prayer book that my wife and I have been using for quite some time. It contains the daily readings for the Mass of the day, morning and evening prayers, as well as a thought-pro-voking reflection. (For more information, write to *Magnificat*, P.O. Box 91, Spencerville, MD 20868-9978; phone 1-800-317-6689; website *www.magnificat.net*.)

One of the most effective prayer tools is a series of books by Francis Fernandez titled *In Conversation with God*, published by Scepter Publishers. These books will provide you with a daily reflection on the liturgical readings throughout the year, with the main focus on the Gospel.

For those of you who prefer the contemplative prayer style, I suggest such fine works as *Imitation of Christ*, by Thomas à Kempis; *Abandonment to Divine Providence*, by Jean-Pierre de Caussade; or any of the works of St. John of the Cross, St. Teresa of Ávila, or Thomas Merton. Please be sure that the Holy Spirit is directing you toward these writings, because they can be very deep and quite confusing at times.

The Rosary

The Rosary has always been one of the most effective prayer tools because we pray to Mary, the Mother of God, who inter-cedes on our behalf with her Son.

When I was in grade school, the sisters taught us to have devotion to Mary through the Rosary. The entire school would say the Rosary one Friday a month. During the month of May, every Friday we would recite the Rosary, followed by a May Crowning.

My devotion to Mary remained through my high school years, and then it began to deteriorate and eventually disappear during my college years. It wasn't until several years after my conversion experience that I revitalized my devotion to the Mother of God. It felt so wonderful and rewarding when I started reciting the Rosary on a regular basis.

I began to realize that it made sense to approach the mother to get to the son. If you think about it, in our personal lives, if somebody needed or wanted something from us and he approached our mother with a request, asking her to intercede with us on his behalf, most of the time, whenever our mother requested anything from us, our answer usually was "Yes." That is why the Rosary has always been such an effective intercessory prayer.

I have been blessed so much by the Rosary that at times I find myself prompted by my Personal Trainer, the Holy Spirit, to give my rosary away. For example, if I'm visiting someone who is ill, or if I'm listening to the troubles of a friend, I'll give them the rosary and encourage them to pray it daily and leave their problems in the hands of the Blessed Virgin.

Of course, these are only suggestions. There are a number of fine prayer books available to aid you during this reflective time. You may ask your Personal Trainer to lead you to the prayer ("tool") book that will be most useful in speaking to your heart.

Prayers of Petition

Finally, I like to go before the Lord with my prayers of petition, asking Him to answer them if it is His will. Our Lord is familiar with each of us, and He will supply us to meet our needs more so than our wants.

For many years, I approached God with propositions. Maybe you can relate to some of these. They went something like this: "Lord, get me through this test . . . through this problem . . . through this illness . . . or get my son or daughter through this particular crisis, and I promise I'll never do this or that again, and I'll start going to confession and attending Mass more often. . . ."

When I was a player in the NFL, I would approach God before kickoff and run this by Him: "O Lord, I know I haven't lived up to the standards You expect of me. In fact, I know I have let You down. But if You permit me to get through this game free from major injury, I promise You that I will turn over a new leaf and become a better Catholic."

Well, this went on for eight years — and God held up His end of the bargain — but I would break my part of the deal within a day or two.

Rather than approaching Our Lord with this childish form of prayer, I now begin my petitions each day by taking inventory of my life, reflecting on the many times I may have offended God in my words and actions, and ask Him for forgiveness — forgiveness for offending Him and my fellow man, in what I have done and what I have failed to do. Once I have completed this first petition and have accepted God's forgiveness, a sense of peace comes over me.

After completing my prayer for forgiveness, I then place before God a list of my petitions. I strongly recommend that you read and reflect on the 17th chapter of John's Gospel. In this chapter, Jesus prays to His Father, asking Him to bless and protect His disciples and all of us in the world.

It is important for us to realize that God is interested not only in our major requests but also in hearing about our seemingly insignificant or unimportant requests. Jesus is interested in everything that we have to say. He can handle our large and small requests with equal ease. Remember, our God is an awesome God, and we shouldn't put limitations on Him. So often we lack sufficient faith to believe that God can and will answer our prayers. All we have to do is ask: "Ask and it will be given to you; seek and you will find; knock and the door will be opened to you. For everyone who asks, receives; and the one who seeks, finds; and to the one who knocks, the door will be opened" (Matthew 7:7-8).

Summary

To summarize, then, my daily format of prayer is made up of the following:

Objectives of Prayer

Hopefully, through my daily stretching out in prayer, God will grant me the grace to fulfill these objectives pertaining to my prayer life:

- To gain a greater desire to know, love, and serve God.
- To strengthen my faith, that I may have confidence that God will answer my prayers.
- To pray that God's will, not mine, be done.
- To help me live a life pleasing to God.
- To always be thankful for the blessings and mercy bestowed on me.
- To attribute the results of prayer solely to the goodness of God.
- To give me the grace to be persistent in prayer.
- To accept whatever happens as the result of divine providence.

Ask the Holy Spirit to direct you to the type of prayer format that will best fit you and your schedule.

Kick Off Your Prayer Time

Now it's time to begin stretching out in prayer. Let's review the four steps to stretching out in prayer:

- First: Make the commitment to pray.
- Second: Take the time to pray.
- Third: Find a place to pray.
- Fourth: Develop a format of prayer.

To echo a famous marketing slogan: "Just do it!"

ACTION PLAN

Things to Do

• Commit to stretching out in prayer on a daily basis.
  Rookie — Pray 10 to 15 minutes a day.
  Veteran — Add five to 10 minutes per month until you
    reach 45 to 60 minutes a day.

Scripture: Luke 18:1

Then he told them a parable about the necessity for them
to pray always without becoming weary. *(You can read
the parable in your Bible, Luke 18:2-8.)*

Run Away From Temptation

Run Toward Jesus!

Jesus spent time in the desert in prayer and fasting following His baptism and before beginning His public ministry. In the desert, He was severely tempted by the devil. You and I are no different. We face temptation and the forces of evil that can destroy our very lives. *You must run away from temptation and run toward Jesus.*

As I mentioned in a previous chapter, the major competition that we face in our spiritual life is against the devil. Satan is the most fierce and cunning competitor that we will ever come up against in our lives. He is a thief, a cheat, a murderer, and a liar — and he does not play by any rules. His main objective is the total destruction of souls. He is "the ancient serpent, who is called the Devil and Satan, who deceived the whole world" (Revelation 12:9).

St. Cyprian, in *De Unitate Ecclesiae*, writes of Satan: "Because he moves silently and seems peaceable and comes by easy ways and is so astute and so deceptive . . . he tries to have night taken for day, poison taken for medicine. So by deception of this kind, he tries to destroy truth by cunning; that is why he passes himself off as an angel of light."

St. Paul tells us that "our struggle is not with flesh and blood but with the principalities, with the powers, with the world rulers of this present darkness, with the evil spirits in the heavens" (Ephesians 6:12).

That is why it is necessary to run toward Jesus, to gather our strength to fight this battle. "Draw your strength from the Lord and from his mighty power. Put on the armor of God so that you may be able to stand firm against the tactics of the devil" (Ephesians 6:10-11).

The game of life is serious business. Every single person on the face of the earth is involved in this competition. The devil has never excluded anyone, including Jesus, from his tactics.

Tempted Like Us

In the Gospels of Matthew (4:1-11) and Luke (4:1-13), we see the utter nerve of Satan when he tries to tempt Jesus. The devil knows that he is dealing with God. He is so cunning that he waits until the end of 40 days, when he knows that Jesus will be hungry and tired, before he begins the temptations. What's even more amazing about this temptation of Jesus is the fact that even when the devil is not successful, he does not give up. St. Luke writes, "When the devil had finished every temptation, he departed from him *for a time*" (Luke 4:13, emphasis added).

If Satan had this much persistence in dealing with Jesus, just imagine the effort that he will put forth to capture our poor souls. The devil will tempt each of us, as he did Jesus, in the hope that we will succumb to His temptations and then sin.

Oh yeah, did you notice in the first part of the Scripture readings who it was that led Jesus into the desert? You guessed it: our Personal Trainer, the Holy Spirit.

The Story of King David

The story of King David and Bathsheba, found in the 11th and 12th chapters of the Second Book of Samuel, is a perfect example of how even a godly king can succumb to the pressures of temptation and sin. It is quite interesting to see how the devil uses one successful temptation to entice David to sin multiple times.

One day David accidentally sees Bathsheba bathing, and he decides he must have her. What makes things worse is that she is the wife of one of his officers who is away at war. After his lust conceives a child, David conceives a cover-up. He calls

Uriah, Bathsheba's husband, home from battle, in the hope that Uriah will have sexual relations with his wife and then think that the child she carries is his. But Uriah spoils the plan, refusing to sleep with Bathsheba out of loyalty to his soldiers who are still fighting a battle, away from their own wives.

The devil tempts David into committing an even greater sin by plotting to have Uriah killed during a battle. Uriah dies as planned. Now David can marry Bathsheba and hide his double sin from all — except from the Lord.

The Lord sends the prophet Nathan to David, and the prophet tells the king a parable and asks him to judge the case. Nathan proceeds to tell David the story about a rich man who had herds in great numbers, and a poor man who had nothing except one little ewe lamb that he had bought. The poor man cherished her as though she were his daughter. The rich man received a visitor and wanted to prepare a meal for him, but he didn't want to take from his own flock. Instead, he took the poor man's ewe lamb to feed the visitor.

David grew angry and interrupted Nathan at this point of the parable to tell him that this rich man deserved to die for what he had done. "Then Nathan said to David: 'You are the man!' . . . Then David said to Nathan, 'I have sinned against the LORD.' Nathan answered David: 'The LORD on his part has forgiven your sin: you shall not die. But since you have utterly spurned the LORD by this deed, the child born to you must surely die'" (2 Samuel 12:7, 13-14).

Even after all of the tragic events of this story about the fall of King David, the Good Lord provides us with hope as we find out later that Solomon, the second child of David and Bathsheba, is favored by the Lord and will be Israel's next king.

Being Forewarned Is Being Forearmed

We must always be alert and on our guard. It is not as though Satan travels around in his devil costume, with a pitchfork, horns, and a long tail dangling behind him. No, evil is too shrewd to give away its disguise. Evil will use the most effective disguise to tempt and then trap every one of us with what allures us. Satan knows our weaknesses better than we do.

Early on in NFL training camps, offensive co-coordinators emphasize to their players how costly mental and physical errors can be when playing the game of football. Let me mention a few of these errors for you:

- Linemen jumping offside in a critical situation.
- Linemen committing holding penalties in the red zone.
- Running backs and wide receivers getting the ball stripped, causing a fumble.
- Broken assignments occurring on a key third-down play.
- Quarterbacks throwing an interception in the red zone.
- Receivers dropping a pass on a possession down.

When these errors happen in the fourth quarter and the game is on the line, they can often make the difference between a team winning or losing. And, of course, it is in the fourth quarter when players tire and lose their focus.

The defense ("the enemy") forces the offense into many of these mistakes by using various tactics, such as:

- Trying to strip the ball, causing a fumble.
- Using quick shift and stunts by the defensive line and linebackers, which cause offensive linemen to either jump offside or miss an assignment.
- Blitzing linebackers or the secondary, which catches the quarterback by surprise, and if he is not alert, forcing him to throw the ball into coverage, causing an interception that can kill a drive.

The best way to prevent these things from happening is by practicing basic fundamental drills each day during practice.

During practice, the defensive unit will utilize all the above tactics that the opponent will use on game day. It is amazing to see what happens to players even after you have harped on these things and practiced them daily. There comes a time when their concentration level drops and — bingo! — a mental or physical error occurs. This causes the "giveaway" ratio to be higher than your "takeaway" ratio, which usually means more losses than wins — and for coaches this spells disaster. I know because I speak from the voice of experience.

The game of life is no different than the game of football. Our ability to play in the fourth quarter will determine whether we reach our goal or fall. Our opponent, the devil, is more than ready to confuse us into making a fatal error.

The Opponent's Confusing Patterns and Disguises

Here are some of the various disguises that the devil likes to use to allure us into sinning.

Pride

The most effective and successful disguise he likes to use is pride. St. Thomas Aquinas, in his *Summa Theologiae*, tells us, "Pride is the mother and root of every sin including mortal sin." Scripture says, "The beginning of pride is man's stubbornness / in withdrawing his heart from his Maker; / For pride is the reservoir of sin" (Sirach 10:12-13). Man is tricked into believing that he really doesn't need God in his life and that he can handle things on his own.

TIME OUT!

Is pride killing you? Let's reflect for a few minutes to see if the devil has been effective in utilizing our pride to infiltrate our thoughts and actions.

Personal

- Men, do you think that the spiritual part of your life is important? Do you even give it a second thought?
- Men, do you attend Sunday Mass, or do you think it's more for women and weak people? (General attendance at Sunday Mass is way off, but for men it is very low.)

Family

- Men, do you believe that you should be the "spiritual head" of the family, or do you leave that role to your wife?
- Men, do you believe that "the family that prays together, stays together," or do you think that this is just an old cliché?
- Men (this question is for all dads), do you realize that your young son loves Mom but wants to be like Dad, and that your example is important? Or do you believe that it won't make a bit of difference in the future spiritual life of your children (especially the boys) whether you participate now in the spiritual life of your family?

Country

- Men, do you realize that either by law or our free choice we have allowed the following things to occur?
  - More than 1 million babies a year are aborted in the United States.
  - Our children are not permitted to pray in our public schools or at sporting events.
  - Some people are trying to remove "under God" from the Pledge of Allegiance.
  - There is a movement to legalize same-sex "marriage."

Church

- Men, do you realize that many Catholics support legalized abortion? Are you one of them?
- Men, do you believe in the real presence of Christ in the Holy Eucharist, or are you like some Catholics who don't?

- Men, do you believe that if you are aware of having committed a moral sin, you cannot receive Holy Communion until you have confessed your sin in the Sacrament of Reconciliation? Or are you like some Catholics who think it doesn't make a difference?

To me, our pride and ego play a major role in all of the above issues. I hate to say this, but I sense that because of our stubbornness in withdrawing our hearts from our Creator, a number of men have come to the conclusion that they don't need God in their lives. Even worse than that, some men don't give it much thought one way or the other.

Consciously or unconsciously, as a nation we have decided to take God out of the family, something which has created so much turmoil and confusion in our marriages and for our children. This is evident in the annual number of divorces in this country, which is almost equal to half the annual number of marriages. This is all part of the devil's plan, because he wants to get the man out of the way so that he can attack the children. It is a simple theory of divide and conquer.

When you take God out of a nation as we are doing, it will inevitably lead to utter destruction. Our country was founded on godly principles, but we have decided that we don't want to hold on to these principles.

The Church is being attacked from all sides, but instead of choosing to "circle the wagons" and band together so that we can put up a good fight, many have used this opportunity to promote their own agendas on how the Church should function. There are thousands of Christian churches in this country, but sadly, many of them are doing things "their way," not "God's way."

Yes, thus far I think the evil one has used "pride" quite successfully to trick man into believing that he really doesn't need God in his life.

Love of Money

Let's continue with another disguise that Satan uses against us — namely, the allurement of riches and money. Scripture tells us, "For the love of money is the root of all evils, and some people in their desire for it have strayed from the faith and have pierced themselves with many pains" (1 Timothy 6:10).

Money in itself is not a problem. But when we become obsessed with it, along with all the material possessions that it can buy and all the power it can exert, we have created a problem.

Money is essential. It is the driving force behind all the economies of the world. Without money, we would not be able to provide social services to the needy or spread the Gospel throughout the world.

But if money is *the goal* that you are living for, you are doomed! As a wise priest, who had preached at many funerals over the years, once said: "In all the funerals that I've been to, I've never seen a hearse towing a U-Haul trailer behind any of them."

The Tongue

The tongue is another disguise that is very difficult to detect, because one minute it can be used to lift up, praise, and encourage others, and the next minute to tear down, judge, and discourage others. On the one hand, in the Book of Sirach, we read: "The LORD has granted me my lips as a reward, / and my tongue will declare his praises" (Sirach 51:22). On the other, the psalmist says: "Your tongue is like a sharpened razor, you skillful deceiver" (Psalm 52:3).

The tongue can produce such a wonderful sound when singing an entertaining song, but it is also capable of blurting out the most vulgar and destructive language. Men, guard your lips, so that it isn't true that "you love any word that destroys, /

you deceitful tongue" (Psalm 52:6). Rather, ask the Lord to open your lips so that you can declare "that my tongue may praise your healing power / . . . [and that] my mouth will proclaim your praise" (Psalm 51:16-17).

Pornography, Drugs, and Alcohol

The most modern disguises of the devil, and probably his most effective weapons against us in this day and age, are pornography and the abuse of drugs and alcohol.

The use of pornography has reached epidemic proportions among men. The devil will use many venues to entice us with his pornographic messages. He uses the various forms of entertainment media that we use and enjoy — such as television, movies, music, books, magazines, and the Internet — to subtly set his snare. It is difficult to acquire accurate records concerning the growth of the pornography industry, but I have heard some estimates that its revenues are close to $10 billon a year.

You are probably wondering how this could be such a huge industry. Simple! It comes down to the old economic theory of supply and demand. If there weren't such a large demand for sex and pornography, the industry eventually would go out of business. Unfortunately, the demand has been so great from their customers (most of whom are men) that the industry continues to grow by leaps and bounds.

Men of all ages are being lured and enticed into this web of deceit, which in many cases leads to an addiction to sex and pornography. Men from every category — from the teenager to the senior citizen, from the single to the married, from the professional to the laborer, and sadly even some of our clergy — are affected.

Drugs and alcohol consumption is on the rise. Police officers and judges will tell you that over 80 percent of all crimes committed are drug- or alcohol-related. The devil uses alcohol and drugs because they wipe away our inhibitions and alter our decision-making process.

I can relate personally to this last statement. Back in my drinking days, on numerous occasions I would promise my wife that I was going to stop partying and settle down — and I really meant it. But soon I would throw down a drink or two, and after that I would say to myself, "Aw, the hell with it," and back out onto the street I went. The devil was whipping me up as though I were a rented donkey.

As you can see, the devil has done a good job selling the idea to men that they can receive all the pleasure and happiness they want in life from sex, pornography, alcohol, and drugs. He has convinced (deceived) so many people into rationalizing that there is nothing wrong with any of this, and that these things are simply ways to make ourselves feel good. Yet the truth is that people are being used and hurt along the way.

There Is Hope!

All of these obstacles can overwhelm us. But do not lose hope! Instead, run toward Jesus, who promises us, "In the world you will have trouble, but take courage, I have conquered the world" (John 16:33).

A Six-Point Game Plan Against Temptation and Sin

➫ First: Fight Back

We must realize that dealing with temptation requires us to put up a helluva fight, and to never give up.

We can always count on Christ's love. Even during the worst moments of our lives, He does not stop loving us. We can always count on His help to return to the right path if we have lost it. He will always help us to begin, and to begin again.

St. John Chrysostom, in his homily on St. Paul's First Letter to the Corinthians, says that a leader on the battlefield places more value on the soldier who, having fallen back in the battle at first, returns to the fray and attacks the enemy with renewed valor than on the soldier who never fled the battle but who also never showed outstanding courage while fighting in it.

◡ Second: Tap Into the Power Source

The strength to defend oneself from the temptation of the evil one comes when we ask Jesus to intercede to the Father on our behalf. This is illustrated so beautifully in Jesus' prayer to the Father, in St. John's Gospel: "I do not ask that you take them out of the world but that you keep them from the evil one" (John 17:15).

How well Jesus understands the human heart, and what a positive conception He has of our abilities! He always understands us and encourages us to continue struggling. If only we could realize Christ's personal love for each of us, as well as His care and solicitude for each one! Jesus always loves us despite the deep-rooted wretchedness that lies in the human heart.

◡ Third: Make Use of God's Support System

Many of us are unaware that God provides each of us with an angel to guard and protect us. In the *Catechism of the Catholic Church*, we read: "From its beginning until death, human life is surrounded by their [guardian angels'] watchful care and intercession (cf. Mt 18:10; Lk 16:22; Ps 34:7; 91:10-13; Job 33:23-24; Zech 1:12; Tob 12:12). 'Beside each believer stands an angel as protector and shepherd leading him to life' (cf. St. Basil, *Adv. Eunomium* III, 1:PG 29, 656B). Already here on earth the Christian life shares by faith in the blessed company of angels and men united in God" (no. 336).

We should call upon the angels to stand watch over our hearts, minds, and bodies. Recall and use the Prayer to St. Michael the Archangel often, especially when you are tempted:

QUOTE

Prayer to St. Michael the Archangel

St. Michael the Archangel, defend us in battle; be our defense against the wickedness and the snares of the devil. May God rebuke him, we humbly pray; and do thou, O prince of the heavenly host, by the power of God, thrust into hell Satan and the other evil spirits who prowl about the world seeking the ruin of souls. Amen.

Jesus gave us His Blessed Mother when He said to the disciple He loved (and that includes all of us), "Behold, your mother" (John 19:27). Approach our heavenly mother, the Blessed Virgin Mary, for support by praying the Rosary and asking her "to pray for us sinners, now and at the hour of our death."

I would like to share with you this lovely prayer about the Blessed Mother:

QUOTE

If the winds of temptation blow,
if you run against the reefs of temptation,
look at the star, call on Mary.
If the waves of pride,
of ambition or of envy are breaking over you,
look at the star,
call on Mary.
If anger, greed or impurity
are violently shaking the ship of your soul,
turn to Mary.
If you are dismayed at the thought of your sins,
confounded by the ugliness of your conscience,

fearful at the idea of judgment
and you begin to sink into a bottomless abyss of sadness
   or of despair,
think about Mary.
When in danger, anguish, or in doubt,
think about Mary, invoke Mary.
Let Mary always be on your lips,
may she never be absent from your heart.
To obtain her help and intercession,
always follow the example of her virtues.
You will not go astray if you follow her.
You will not despair if you call to her.
You will not get lost if you think about her.
If she is protecting you, you have nothing to fear.
You will not grow weary if she is your guide.
You will reach port safely if she is looking after you.

ST. BERNARD OF CLAIRVAUX

⇨ Fourth: Call for Help

We must realize that we cannot overcome the power of temptation on our own, but that it can be accomplished only with God's help. We only have to reflect on our many failures to have this point driven home for us.

Let me share with you this wonderful meditation on divine strength:

QUOTE

Sometimes we hear this lament: "I would like to correct my faults, to improve myself, but I just can't!" But then we read that even throughout the centuries there existed leaders and successful men and women who could not dominate their evil inclinations. That was, for instance, the case of Alexander the Great, who died prematurely due to the looseness of his life. Taking a look around us, we observe the disappearance of our moral standards. We are witnessing the creation of diabolic associations, which have included crime and dissoluteness in their agenda. How can we counter this? To admit one's own powerlessness in such circumstances could appear to be humility, such as the phrase, "I am not able to correct myself." In reality, it is only concealed pride. Why? Because people often admit they have the ability to do some things, but then they say they cannot repress a given fault, avoid a given circumstance. This only proves that they only count on their own strength to master their lives. But this is a false concept, since with our sole strength, just by ourselves without God's help, we can do nothing, absolutely nothing (see John 15:5). The truth is that all that we are and have or are able to do, it is thanks to God, who gives these things to us constantly. In fact, we exist because God is giving and supporting our existence at every moment. Therefore, by ourselves we can do nothing, except evil, which is in fact a lack of good, of order, of power. If we acknowledge this truth and turn our eyes to God, from whom we receive all that we are at every instant of our lives, we would see at once that there is much more He can give us, and that, as the best of Fathers, He wants to give us whatever we need.

St. Maximilian Kolbe

➯ Fifth: Place Your Hope in God

In Psalm 51, the famous *Miserere*, one of the most powerful psalms, there are strong and dramatic phrases that show in all seriousness and gravity the limit and fragility of the human creature, man's perverse capacity to sow evil and violence, impurity and falsehood. However, the message of the *Miserere* is this: God can "cancel, wash, clean" the fault that is confessed with a contrite heart. We hear King David, a converted sinner (remember Uriah's wife and what David did to Uriah?), pray: "Have mercy on me, God, in your goodness; / in your abundant compassion blot out my offense. / Wash away all my guilt; / from my sin cleanse me" (Psalm 51:3-4).

In the Book of Isaiah, we hear the Lord speak: "Though your sins be like scarlet, / they may become white as snow; / Though they be crimson red, / they may become white as wool," (Isaiah 1:18).

The *Imitation of Christ*, a text so dear to the Christian spiritual tradition, repeats the same admonition as the psalmist: "The humble contrition of sins is for you the pleasing sacrifice, a perfume more delicate than the smoke of incense. In it, every iniquity is purified and washed."

⮑ Sixth: Undergo a Spiritual Exam and Confess Your Sins

Original sin came into the world through the fall of Adam and Eve. We also know that the Sacrament of Baptism totally wipes away all of our sins, including original sin. Yet, we continue to live in a fallen world and are sinners. As St. John tells us, "If we say, 'We are without sin,' we deceive ourselves, and the truth is not in us" (1 John 1:8).

Whenever we come down with some kind of physical ailment or whenever we start a new exercise program, medical experts strongly suggest that we get checked out by undergoing a physical exam. As a result of this exam, the doctor is able to determine the cause of our ailment, and then prescribe the proper medication to help us regain our health; the results of this exam will also determine whether we should start an exercise program.

The Sacrament of Reconciliation — also known as the Sacrament of Penance or simply as "confession" — has long been suggested by the Church as a way for Catholics to become "spiritually fit." Jesus instituted this sacrament in order to provide us with a way of getting rid of all the spiritual ailments, or sins, in our life. The *Catechism of the Catholic Church* has a complete and thorough explanation of the Sacrament of Penance (nos. 1422-1498).

For many years, the notion of sin has been often avoided by people calling sin everything else but sin. The issue has been skirted and evaded long enough. It is now time to realize that sin is part of our lives, and that we can deal with it by utilizing all the means provided to us by the Catholic Church.

Overcoming Fear

In my conversations with people, especially men, about the Sacrament of Reconciliation and why they have a hard time going, it seems that their big hang-up is confessing their sins personally to a priest. The best explanation that I can give comes from the words of Jesus in St. John's Gospel: "[Jesus] said to them again, 'Peace be with you. As the Father has sent me, so I send you.' And when he had said this, he breathed on them and said to them, 'Receive the holy Spirit. Whose sins you forgive are forgiven them, and whose sins you retain are retained' " (John 20:21-23). In other words, this is what the Scriptures tell us is the will of God. Jesus gave men the power to forgive sins!

When I was growing up, confession was always held behind a screen in a confessional box. Many of us liked this because the priest could not see us and we could disguise our voices. At St. Peter's Grade School, we started to have confessions once a month for the entire school for those who were of age. It started to take too long, so the Dominican sisters invited several more priests to participate. Because of the shortage of confessionals, two of the priests had to hear confessions face-to-face at the altar.

We didn't have an option regarding which priest we confessed to back in those days — but, of course, everyone wanted to avoid those two priests at the altar like the plague. Well, you guessed it: I was chosen to go to one of those priests. The one I got stuck with was from our parish — and he was hard of hearing!

It was my worst nightmare come true. I started to whisper my sins, rather rapidly. But one that he heard must have struck a nerve, because he stopped me and blurted out loudly, echoing throughout the church: "YOU DID WHAT?" When I was finished and turned around, my face was red as scarlet. It seemed as though the whole school was looking at me and that they had heard my confession.

From that day on, and for many years after, I made sure I went to confession only in "the box." Eventually, I came to realize that it doesn't make a difference which form I use: face-to-face or behind a screen. And it doesn't make any difference which priest I choose, because the priest represents Jesus Christ and can absolve our sins.

The *Catechism* (no. 1496) lists the spiritual effects of the Sacrament of Reconciliation. Read through this list and reflect on all these benefits. Then you will see why my wife and I make it a point to go to confession once a month.

Recently, in the Archdiocese of New Orleans, we held a Morning of Spirituality for Catholic Men with Archbishop Alfred Hughes. We were very pleased, because some 800 men attended the first event.

As part of the program, we decided to set aside approximately one hour for the men to have an opportunity to go to confession. Prior to beginning the confessions, we arranged to have a diocesan priest present a short reflection on the examination of conscience. This was very helpful to the men, especially to the ones who hadn't been to confession in quite some time. Around 35 priests were there to administer the sacrament, which turned out to be a true blessing, because over 65 percent of the men went to confession. Many of the men had not been to confession in 10, 20, or 30 years. The word got back to us that there were two reasons why so many men went to confession that particular day:

1. Men saw other men going to confession, and it inspired them to go, even though they hadn't done so in years.
2. Men mentioned that they had time not only to confess their sins but also to *discuss* their sins.

My personal opinion is that the Holy Spirit, the Personal Trainer, was at full force that particular morning.

Still Need Help?

If you have not been to confession for a long time or don't remember how to go to confession, contact your parish priest or any priest that you feel comfortable with, and he will guide you through the process.

TIME OUT!

Why not consider making a promise to the Lord that you will return to the Sacrament of Reconciliation?

One last vital item concerning confession, which is critical for making a good confession, is to make a firm commitment to not sin again. The Catholic Church provides us with a wonderful prayer that we can say after we confess our sins:

QUOTE

Act of Contrition

O my God, I am heartily sorry for having offended you, and I detest all my sins because of your just punishments, but most of all because they offend you, my God, who are all good and deserving of all my love. I firmly resolve, with the help of your grace, to sin no more and to avoid the near occasions of sin. Amen.

I would like to close out this chapter with a quote from Pope John Paul II: "Knowing that we are reconciled with God and filled with hope, let us pray for the courage to proclaim to the world His praises, and let us teach others the reconciliation and forgiveness of our loving God."

ACTION PLAN

Things to Do
- Make a thorough examination of conscience.
- Go to confession if you have not been doing so. (The ultimate goal is monthly confession.)

Scripture: 2 Corinthians 5:20
We implore you on behalf of Christ, be reconciled to God.

STEP FIVE

Lift Up Others in Prayer

Being a Man for Others

The one positive thing that has come out of the terrorist attacks against the World Trade Center, the Pentagon, and Flight 93 is that people basically do love and care about one another. Unfortunately, it often takes a horrible tragedy like 9/11 to bring out those qualities in us. We saw and heard of tremendous heroics by so many people who risked or gave their lives for others, most of whom had never met each other before that day.

These tremendously uplifting stories of people helping to lift up other people should be a wonderful witness that we need to carry over into our own personal lives. If you are going to lead a spiritual life, you are going to have to be a "man for others." This involves doing some heavy lifting — in this case, it means lifting others up in prayer. It also means giving them a helping hand. Jesus said: "Love one another. As I have loved you, so you also should love one another. This is how all will know that you are my disciples, if you have love for one another" (John 13:34-35).

Whom do we need to "lift up"? Who needs our help?

Elderly Parents

Sadly, today we hear of many cases of adult children who don't get along with their parents, or in some cases don't even speak to them. A visit to the local nursing home will reveal elderly parents who are never visited by their adult children. The fourth commandment says, "Honor your father and your mother, that you may have a long life in the land which the

LORD, your God, is giving you"(Exodus 20:12). *The Catechism of the Catholic Church* states: "Respecting this commandment provides, along with spiritual fruits, temporal fruits of peace and prosperity. Conversely, failure to observe it brings great harm to communities and to individuals" (no. 2200).

My brother recently shared with me an article on senior citizens that appeared in a national newspaper. It reported that within the next 10 to 12 years 50 percent of our nation's population will be over 69 years of age, with seniors as the fastest-growing age group.

I believe that elderly parents deserve to be treated with the utmost respect and dignity by their adult children. Elderly parents have earned this because of the many years they have dedicated to their children. Even more important than my opinion is God's command that children should love their parents.

The Catholic Church teaches that grown children still have responsibilities to their parents. We must, to the best of our ability, take care of them, both materially and spiritually, in their time of need (see *Catechism of the Catholic Church*, no. 2218). Scripture tells us this: "My son, take care of your father when he is old; / grieve him not as long as he lives. / Even if his mind fail, be considerate with him; / revile him not in the fullness of your strength. / ... A blasphemer is he who despises his father; / accursed of his Creator, he who angers his mother" (Sirach 3:12-13, 16).

TIME OUT!

Spend some time thinking about the following:

- Is there an elderly friend or a family member that I am neglecting? Lift that person up to God in prayer right now. Ask your Personal Trainer, the Holy Spirit, to give you the zeal to either pick up the phone and give them a call or visit them.

My Parents' Example

When I was a child, we moved several times to different neighborhoods within my hometown. The first place that I can remember was 1158 Sycamore Street — the home of my great-grandparents, Skeets and Katherine Kelly. My parents took care of this old, sick couple until the death of Great-Grandpa Skeets, who had a long bout with cancer. After his death, my mom's mom thought it would be better if she would move into the house so that she could take care of her mother, Great-Grandma Kelly. It was an inconvenience for our family to move out and allow my grandmother to move in, but we did it because my mom loved and honored her mother.

I enjoyed living at that home for two good reasons. First of all, Skeets would send me off each day to buy him a pint of whiskey, and in return he would give me a bunch of candy that he had hidden. One day I happened to see where he had the candy stored — so whenever he dozed off in his chair, my brother and I would sneak into his room and ransack the candy.

Secondly, whenever my dad paddled me, I made sure I cried as loud as I possibly could so that Great-Grandma Kelly would hear me and come down the stairs and give my dad absolute hell.

All of this brings up another reason to stay connected to your elderly family members: Your children need to know these pillars of your family.

Spouse

While it is important and necessary to love our children, it is vital that husband and wife love and respect each other.

As the man of the house, our role as father is to lift up our family. The first person that we need to lift up and affirm is our spouse, because she will be with us long after our children have gone off on their own. St. Paul writes: "Be subordinate to one another out of reverence for Christ. Wives should be subordinate to their husbands as to the Lord.... So [also] husbands should love their wives as their own bodies. He who loves his wife loves himself.... / 'For this reason a man shall leave [his] father and [his] mother / and be joined to his wife, / and the two shall become one flesh'" (Ephesians 5:21-22, 28, 31).

So many times in marriage, spouses take each other for granted, especially if they have been married for a number of years. On their wedding day, they professed marriage vows, saying that they accepted each other "for better, for worse, for richer, for poorer, in sickness and in health, until death do us part." Today, in our society, with its catastrophic divorce rate, it seems as though spouses have been tearing each other down instead of lifting each other up.

Earlier, I shared with you the story of my addiction to alcohol and how that had placed a tremendous strain on my marriage. But my wife lifted me up through the power of prayer, and by the grace of God we were able to overcome this trial. Just think what could have happened if my wife hadn't held true to our wedding vows and if she hadn't lifted me up in prayer. God only knows where I would have ended up — probably dead. On August 20, 2003, my wife and I celebrated our 37th wedding anniversary.

TIME OUT!

I believe there are some very practical ways for spouses to lift each other up in their marriage. Men, take some time to do the following:

- Begin by acknowledging the beauty of your wife and telling her how much you love her. Let her know how

much you appreciate her as the mother of your children — oops! I mean God's children. Watch her eyes light up and a big smile come across her face. Finally, take her in your arms and give her a big kiss and a hug.
- Make sure to "date" your wife at least once a week. Keep the romance alive in your marriage!

Taking my wife out on a date once a week, usually for dinner, does wonders for both of us. I realize that many of you young dads have families with small children, and that it can be difficult to find the time. But I still think it is necessary for you to figure out a way to find a baby-sitter so that you and your wife can go on a date, to grab a hamburger and then go to a movie. If push comes to shove, at least go out for coffee and dessert.

I would like to suggest one last thing that is very difficult but also very effective in strengthening relationships and very uplifting. Ask each other for forgiveness whenever a misunderstanding has arisen and an argument has occurred. Many times all that is required is to say, "I'm sorry."

Sometimes my wife will walk over to me and say, "I know that you want to tell me you are sorry for yelling at me." We both start laughing. So, whether you think you are right or wrong (and men, you know that we're always right — but don't let your wife see this!), I urge you to take the lead and ask your wife for her forgiveness. (Do you want to know the real truth? My wife is right most of the time!) Before using this approach, however, I do suggest that you wait a little while, to let things cool down, or the whole argument could erupt again.

I've noticed in our marriage — and also by talking with our married friends — that some of the major problems occur when both parities use the "silent treatment." It is critical for married couples to always keep the lines of communication open. It's not a matter of *whether* a disagreement is going to take place in our marriages but *when*. Whenever it does happen, we must be open to dialogue and discussion. It should not be a time for arguing and shouting and belittling one another.

Duties of Family

As the fathers of our homes, we men must be aware of our duties as parents. The *Catechism of the Catholic Church* does a wonderful job outlining parental responsibilities:

- First, we must treat our children as children of God, just as we are. We need to make this clear to them and educate them in the faith so that their lives are lived in obedience to God's commands (see no. 2222).
- Second, we should make our homes places "where tenderness, forgiveness, respect, fidelity, and disinterested service are the rule. The home is well suited for *education in the virtues*" (no. 2223).
- Third, we have a duty as parents to teach our children how to pray and discover the gifts and talents that God has blessed them with, and how they can serve God in their vocation in life (see no. 2226).
- Fourth, "Parents' respect and affection are expressed by the care and attention they devote to bringing up their young children and *providing for their physical and spiritual needs*" (no. 2228).

Dads, I would like to address the topic of affection (love) that was mentioned in the previous paragraph. Some fathers acknowledge that they have a very difficult time showing affection (love) to their children, especially to their boys. Many men will tell me that their children already know that they love them. My response is, "How do you know that? Do you tell them that you love them? Do you hug them and kiss them? Do you give them your full attention?"

I'm amazed by the number of men that respond "no" to these questions.

TIME OUT!

Men, if you don't get anything else out of this book except what I am about to say, I will be happy:

- I want all of you fine men, regardless of what has happened in the past, to put this book down right now and go over to your children and tell each one how much *you love him or her* and give each a *big hug* and a *kiss*. It doesn't matter how old they are. Kiss and hug the boys, too.

My boys are 36 and 33, and we use a handshake along with a kiss and a hug when we greet each other. My father is 84 years old and my father-in-law is 79, and we greet each other the same way.

Maybe some of you dads are faced with the situation that you and your son are not speaking. It's time for you to change this. You need to love him, and to show your love, even if it means getting in your car and driving over to his home — or if he lives out of town, calling him on the phone. Do it right now! Life is way too short to live this way.

Another critical factor in our relationship with our children is our availability. Children will approach us at the most unlikely times looking for our advice and attention.

In this day and age when both parents work to provide the good things in life, we miss opportunities to bond with our children. When we come home from work, we are either too exhausted or our minds are out in left field somewhere instead of focused on the family. The dad plops down in a chair, with a beer in his hand, and turns the television on. Low and behold, his son comes up and wants to talk, but the old man has one eye on the boy and one eye on the TV. You can be darn sure his mind is not on what the boy is saying, because the boy has just told the dad he blew up the school today, and the dad replies, "That's good, Son!"

This may be somewhat of an exaggeration, but I don't think it's far from the truth. Our children are sharp, and they know whether we are giving them our full attention or just a bunch of lip service. The most awesome responsibility we have in this life is the rearing of our children, because in the end we must go before God and account for how we raised *His children.*

Relatives and Friends

In addition to lifting up our immediate family members, we must be open to lifting up our relatives and friends. Jesus said to His disciples: "I give you a new commandment: love one another. As I have loved you, so you also should love one another" (John 13:34).

In some families, relatives won't even speak to one another: Brothers won't speak to brothers, one uncle won't speak to another uncle, or in-laws don't get along with other in-laws. I know of people who had been very close friends for years, but because of some disagreement are now bitter enemies. If you really think about it, life is too short to allow some silly misunderstanding to destroy a relationship with a relative or friend. Sadly, many of these disagreements are over money.

I recall an incident that occurred several years ago between two elderly aunts of mine. Both of them were wonderful Catholic women whom I loved and respected very much. But one day my dad mentioned to me that his two sisters were not talking to each other because of some difference that had occurred between the two of them. This really upset me, so I began to pray and ask God to intervene in this situation. It was particularly disturbing because both of them were quite old; in fact, one of them was beginning to have major health problems. Finally, one day during my prayer time, the Lord put on my heart the thought to call both of my aunts. I asked my Personal Trainer for the courage and the guidance to handle this matter.

The next day I placed a long distance call to each of them. I told them that I loved them very much, and that I was aware of their disagreement and the fact that they were not speaking to each other.

Basically, I told them that no matter the reason for this disagreement, God did not want them to live out their remaining time on this earth separated from each other. I also said that one of them must go to see the other and apologize, and that God would heal this hurt. I then said that one of them would have to deal with a tremendous amount of guilt for the rest of her life if this relationship did not get straightened out before one of them passed away. Lastly, the Lord gave me the strength to pray with each of them.

Several days later, I received a phone call from both of them telling me that they were happily together again. I thanked the Good Lord for inspiring me to lift up both of my aunts.

To put a wonderful close to this story, I must share with you that one of these aunts did pass away approximately one year after their reunion. The surviving aunt wrote and thanked me for patching up their relationship.

My response: Don't thank me. Thank God.

Others

I work in a high-rise building in downtown New Orleans. When I get on the elevator every morning or when I walk the streets during lunchtime, I notice many people that need to be lifted up, men and women with sad and drawn faces. I see people that don't seem to be very hospitable.

On the other hand, I do see people riding the elevator with smiles on their faces, saying, "Good morning." This lifts up everyone there. People on the street that are polite and hospitable can influence other people around them in a positive way. Our society — especially the news media — has a tendency to focus on the negative, instead of the positive. The world tends to whip people down, not lift them up.

TIME OUT!

Our own personal attitude can make a big difference in our life and in the lives of the people we come in contact with, especially our co-workers. Here's an exercise to try, with a "misery back" guarantee:

- Try this for the next 30 days, both at home and at work. Put a smile on your face, place a bounce in your step, add a positive tone to your voice, and watch the difference all of this will make. If, after 30 days, you don't see a big difference in your life, you can have your misery back.

Our Enemies

The hardest people to lift up in life are our enemies. Lifting up our loved ones is not that difficult; lifting up a person who has done us an injustice is very difficult. But Jesus tells us that we must lift up our enemies. Sometimes this is easier said than done.

In 1984, the World's Fair came to New Orleans. Prior to its opening, the fair was being touted as a bonanza for the city and for all its investors.

A close friend of mine persuaded me to make a large investment in two projects with him and some other men. The first investment was a large hotel near the World's Fair site, and the second was a large gondola ride that would expand across the Mississippi River, with the entrance to this ride close to our hotel. I was assured that I would have only limited liability, and that these were "can't miss" projects.

The estimates of the number of people that would attend the fair were astronomical. The pre-fair publicity was great, up to a point. Then word filtered out that the construction of the fair was way behind schedule and that many people were canceling their reservations. The real truth was that the fair was basically on schedule and that only a few small projects were behind. Of course, the news media picked up the story that the fair was woefully behind schedule and wouldn't open on time.

This negative publicity really had a dramatic effect on attendance at the fair, from start to finish. The actual attendance numbers were far fewer than originally estimated, and this resulted in financial problems for many investors, including us — big time! After the fair, one thing led to another, in each of these investments, until the lending institutions started closing in on us.

I'll never forget the night I received a registered letter stating that I needed to come up with a large chunk of cash, in order to pay my portion of the monthly losses. It also said that if I didn't put up my share, I would forfeit a portion of my percentage in the projects.

The next morning I contacted my friend to find out what the hell was going on. He said that both projects were losing money and that the lending institutions were coming after us. I mentioned to him that I thought we had limited liability. He replied that he didn't remember saying that, and then he asked if I had ever read the closing documents. Of course, I hadn't read them; they were the size of a large dictionary. But more importantly, I had trusted his word.

Finally, to make a long story short, after several lawsuits that I had filed were settled, I walked away with a wallet that was bare and a heart full of anger and resentment. This man and I did not speak to each other for over 15 years. Even though along the way in my spiritual journey I was able to forgive this man, I knew that eventually I would have to personally forgive him, face-to-face, to clear this from my heart.

It is amazing how God's hand works in these situations. A mutual friend called to tell me that this fellow's daughter was battling cancer, and he gave me his phone number. My Personal Trainer, the Holy Spirit, spoke to my heart. So I called this man and said how sorry I was to hear about his daughter, and I asked him if it would be okay if I prayed for her over the phone. He said yes. When I was finished, I told him that I forgave him for the hurt he had caused me and my family, and I apologized for any harm I had caused him and his family. He began to cry, and he apologized and said how much he missed me.

Several weeks later, all of us got together at his house for dinner. We still stay in contact — although you can be sure that we won't be going into any business deals together!

Anyway, that's why it is so necessary to *pray* and *ask* the Holy Spirit to give us the inner strength to forgive those people who have gravely hurt us. Remember Jesus' answer to Peter when he asked the Lord how often he had to forgive: "I say to you, not seven times but seventy-seven times" (Matthew 18:22). In other words, as many times as necessary.

Priests and Religious

Today, those in the greatest need of being lifted up are our priests and religious. Priests and religious have been much maligned over the last few years, and it's time for this bashing to stop. At times, some criticisms directed at priests and religious may have been justified, but by and large they have served our Church very honorably.

The greatest calling on the face of this earth is to the priesthood. We must acknowledge the work these men do by telling them that we love them, and that we appreciate all that they do for us. I believe that it is even more important that men lift up their parish priest and make him feel that he is "one of the guys."

No offense to women is intended here, but what has happened in many parishes is that priests have been surrounded by too many women. They need the association with other men. Women are around the priest because they are the ones accomplishing much of the work in the parish. The men are either not attending church or not interested in getting involved.

Many have wondered why the numbers of vocations have fallen off so dramatically in the last decade or so. It's very simple: Parents have not lifted up vocations to the priesthood or religious life as viable options for their children. We want our children to become doctors, lawyers, or business executives, but the notion of becoming a priest or religious never enters into the equation.

In fact, I have heard the case of a child mentioning to his father that he was thinking about becoming a priest, and the father almost went through the roof. He said to his son: "You don't want to do that with your life! Besides, do you have any idea what kind of money they get paid?"

If we start lifting up priests and religious to their rightful places, I think we will begin to see an increase in vocations.

Let me tell you how my wife and I feel about our oldest son, as this pertains to vocations. If God calls this man to the priesthood, we will be the happiest parents on the face of this earth.

Be a Light in the Darkness

This beautiful Scripture passage from Matthew's Gospel encourages men to be a light in a dark world, so that we can lift up others: "You are the light of the world. A city set on a mountain cannot be hidden. Nor do they light a lamp and then put it under a bushel basket; it is set on a lampstand, where it gives light to all in the house. Just so, your light must shine before others, that they may see your good deeds and glorify your heavenly Father" (Matthew 5:14-16).

ACTION PLAN

Things to Do

- Do something with your wife that she will enjoy.
- Spend more time listening to your children.
- Tell your parish priest how much you appreciate him.

Scripture: John 15:17

"This I command you: love one another."

STEP SIX

Receive Your Spiritual Nutrition

Getting a Healthy Spiritual Diet

Our society is more nutrition-conscious now than at any other time in our history. Billions of dollars are spent each year by the general public on various nutritional supplements and on specialized diets that help strengthen and build up our bodies. Athletes at all levels are becoming more and more aware of the importance of a balanced nutritional program and how it can enhance their performance.

In most physical fitness workout programs, instructors recommend that participants maintain a proper nutritional diet of some form. If they do not maintain this proper nutrition, they will begin to weaken, and they will not be able to derive all of the benefits from the physical workouts.

It is not only important that we nourish our physical bodies, but it is also essential that we nourish our minds and hearts (souls).

We feed our minds with the basic skills of reading, writing, and math. If you were like me growing up, at times I learned those basic skills from the sisters to the tune of a hickory stick.

We must nourish ourselves spiritually in order to build up our hearts with faith, hope, and charity. If we fail to provide our souls with the proper nutrition, our spiritual life will dwindle away to nothing, and quite possibly it could cause us to become spiritually dead.

The two most effective sources of spiritual nutrition are, first and foremost, the Holy Eucharist and, second, the Word of God.

The Holy Eucharist

Rather than beat around the bush, let's cut right to the chase and refer to the Scriptures to see what Jesus has to say about the Eucharist in regards to our personal spiritual nutrition:

QUOTES

"I am the living bread that came down from heaven; whoever eats this bread will live forever; and the bread that I will give is my flesh for the life of the world."

JOHN 6:51

"Whoever eats my flesh and drinks my blood has eternal life, and I will raise him on the last day."

JOHN 6:54

"Whoever eats my flesh and drinks my blood remains in me and I in him."

JOHN 6:56

The *Catechism of the Catholic Church* states that the Eucharist is " 'the source and summit of the Christian life (*LG* 11)' " (no. 1324). It also notes that " 'the other sacraments, and indeed all ecclesiastical ministries and works of the apostolate, are bound up with the Eucharist and are oriented toward it. For in the blessed Eucharist is contained the whole spiritual good of the Church, namely Christ himself, our Pasch' (*PO* 5) " (no. 1324).

In the Constitution on the Sacred Liturgy, the Second Vatican Council declared that everything that the Church does is directed toward the Eucharist, and that there is no activity of the Church that is more important than celebrating this sacrament (see no. 7).

Structure of the Eucharist/Mass

The *Catechism of the Catholic Church* explains the basic structure for the Eucharist/Mass:

QUOTE

The liturgy of the Eucharist/Mass unfolds according to a fundamental structure which has been preserved throughout the centuries down to our own day. It displays two great parts that form a fundamental unity:

— the gathering, the liturgy of the Word, with readings, homily, and general intercessions;

— the liturgy of the Eucharist, with the presentation of the bread and wine, the consecratory thanksgiving, and communion.

The liturgy of the Word and liturgy of the Eucharist together form "one single act of worship" (cf. *SC 56*); the Eucharistic table set for us is the table both of the Word of God and of the Body of the Lord (cf. *DV 21*).

CATECHISM OF THE CATHOLIC CHURCH, NO. 1346

The term "Mass" (*Missa*) comes from the final words of the priest at the end of the liturgy: in Latin, "*Ite, missa est*" (literally, "Go, you are sent!"). Going to Mass is all about being nourished to go back out into our day-to-day world to do the will of God.

Jogging to Mass

On a cold winter's morning in 1955, I jogged from my home in the north end of town to St. Peter's Convent, to serve my first Mass that began at 5:45. It was a difficult task jogging two miles to the convent that early in the morning, in the cold, but that was easy compared to serving Mass in front of all the Dominican sisters, especially in front of Sister Mary Dennis, who had taught me the Latin responses. Besides all that, I found out that Monsignor Grigsby, the pastor, would be celebrating the Mass.

I had hardly slept a wink the night before, for fear that my mom's alarm would not go off in time and I would arrive late. As you might have guessed, I had already started dressing when my mom came to my room. As far as the "jog" to Mass was concerned, I was so nervous that I think I sprinted the entire distance.

I arrived at the back door of the convent, huffing and puffing, and rang the doorbell. Who do you think answered the door? Yeah, you guessed it: Sister Mary Dennis. She immediately directed me to the sacristy, where I vested for Mass. After vesting, I walked out to the altar, and much to my surprise the small chapel was filled with sisters. The pews were very close to the altar, and Sister Mary Dennis was seated in the first row, close to me, so that she could hear me recite my Latin prayers.

When Mass began, and it was time for my first Latin response, my mind went totally blank! Sister Mary Dennis tapped (rapped!) me on the head and primed me by giving me the first couple of words to get me started. This procedure continued throughout most of that Mass. I was never so glad to have something over with, when finally, Monsignor and I genuflected, left the altar, and went back into the sacristy.

Once we arrived in the sacristy, Monsignor Grigsby immediately told me what a good job I had done. A few minutes later, Sister Mary Dennis approached me to say that she thought I did quite well, and that all I really needed to do was brush up on my Latin prayers. I was so proud that I jogged all the way back home to tell my mom and dad. I served Mass in the convent for the following two weeks. At the end of the two-week period, Sister Mary Dennis informed me that I was now prepared to serve Mass in the main church.

Priests and religious were my main teachers during my elementary and high school days. As a result of this, we were drilled in the basic fundamentals of our Catholic faith. As students, we attended Mass frequently. Although we didn't understand everything that was going on, because of the Latin, we still had a profound reverence for the Mass. If we got out of line during Mass, the sisters would discipline us and teach us to have the proper respect for what was occurring on the altar.

The Mass that I served 46 years ago at St. Peter's Convent and the Mass that my wife and I attend today at St. Patrick's Church in New Orleans are the same Mass, except for the Latin language. Both Masses consist of the Liturgy of the Word and the Liturgy of the Eucharist. In fact, every Mass offered this day and every day around the world is the same, except for the language, which varies, depending on the country or culture.

It is utterly amazing to realize that every single time a priest recites the words of consecration at Mass, the bread and wine are changed into the Body and Blood of Jesus Christ, and that these are the words our Lord and Savior recited to the apostles at the Last Supper, when He instituted the Sacrament of the Eucharist:

QUOTE

While they were eating, Jesus took bread, said the blessing, broke it, and giving it to his disciples said, "Take and eat; this is my body." Then he took a cup, gave thanks, and gave it to them, saying, "Drink from it, all of you, for this is my blood of the covenant, which will be shed on behalf of many for the forgiveness of sins."

MATTHEW 26:26-28; also see MARK 14:22-24
and LUKE 22:19-20

The Real Presence of Jesus

From recent surveys of Catholics in the United States, some alarming statistics have been revealed. Fewer than half — perhaps as few as 35 percent — of all Catholics attend Sunday Mass regularly. An even more shocking finding is that 50 percent or more of all Catholics do not believe in the real presence of Jesus in the Eucharist — and some of these unbelievers are priests.

Pope Paul VI addressed this issue, when he wrote: "The Fathers felt they had a solemn duty to warn the faithful that, in reflecting upon this most sacred Sacrament, they should not pay attention to the senses, which report only the properties of bread and wine, but rather to the words of Christ, which have power great enough to change, transform, 'transelementize' the bread and wine into His body and blood. As a matter of fact, as the same Fathers point out on more than one occasion, the power that does this is the same power of Almighty God that created the whole universe out of nothing at the beginning of time" (*Mysterium Fidei*, no. 47).

The *Catechism* also teaches this: " 'That in this sacrament are the true Body of Christ and his true Blood is something that "cannot be apprehended by the senses," says St. Thomas, *but only by faith,* which relies on divine authority." For this reason, in a commentary on Luke 22:19 ("This is my body which is given for you"), St. Cyril says: "Do not doubt whether this is true, but rather receive the words of the Savior in faith, for since he is the truth, he cannot lie" ' (St. Thomas Aquinas, *STh* III, 75, 1; cf. Paul VI, *MF* 18; St. Cyril of Alexandria, *In Luc.* 22, 19: PG 72, 912; cf. Paul VI, *MF* 18)" (no. 1381).

Additional Nutrition

In my personal life, I began attending Mass and receiving the Eucharist on a daily basis about 12 years ago. My wife also attends Mass and receives the Eucharist daily.

This is not something that happened easily and without some struggle. For many years, I was a Catholic who played it by the book, as it pertained to the Mass and the Eucharist. I always was within the prescribed guidelines set forth by the Church. In fact, I would attend Mass each Sunday and receive the Eucharist once or twice a month. But I would attend Mass during the week only on special occasions.

Once I began to take the spiritual part of my life more seriously, I sensed an urge inside me to become closer to Jesus. I suddenly realized that the best way to satisfy this hunger for Jesus was through the Eucharist. So I began receiving the Eucharist each Sunday, not because of some Church law, but because I wanted and needed to do it. I started attending Mass during the week — and the days I was not attending Mass, I noticed a definite difference. So, through the grace of God, I began attending Mass on a daily basis.

As a result, my life has never been the same. I thank the Good Lord for granting me the opportunity to personally receive Him each day. I really mean this from the bottom of my heart. Each day I can't wait to jog to Mass!

Necessity of This Spiritual Nutrition

In the same way that bodily food is necessary for life on earth, Holy Communion is necessary for maintaining the life of the soul, which is why the Church exhorts us to receive this sacrament frequently. Pope Paul VI explained it this way: "It is desirable to have the faithful in large numbers take an active part in the sacrifice of the Mass each and every day and receive the nourishment of Holy Communion with a pure and holy mind and offer fitting thanks to Christ the Lord for such a great gift. They should remember these words: 'The desire of Jesus Christ and of the Church to see all the faithful approach the sacred banquet each and every day is based on a wish to have them all united to God through the Sacrament and to have them draw from it the strength to master their passions, to wash away the lesser sins that are committed every day and to prevent the serious sins to which human frailty is subject' (Decree of the Sacred

Congregation of the Council, December 20, 1905)" (*Mysterium Fidei*, no. 66).

TIME OUT!

Here is a challenge for you:

- I urge you to pray to your Personal Trainer, the Holy Spirit, to instill in you the desire to attend Mass and receive Holy Communion on a more frequent basis. Maybe it's been quite some time since you attended Mass and received the Eucharist. That's okay! God will understand. He wants you to come back home to Him. Ask Him. I promise you that He will never deny you your wish to receive Him in the Eucharist.

Being Prepared

Just as we wouldn't eat a regular meal without washing our hands, so there are certain things that are necessary in order to receive Holy Communion. We must follow certain precepts of the Church, as pointed out in the *Catechism of the Catholic Church*:

QUOTES

The Church warmly recommends that the faithful receive Holy Communion when they participate in the celebration of the Eucharist; she obliges them to do so at least once a year.

CATECHISM OF THE CATHOLIC CHURCH, NO. 1417

Anyone who desires to receive Christ in Eucharistic communion must be in the state of grace. Anyone aware of having sinned mortally must not receive communion without having received absolution in the sacrament of penance.

CATECHISM OF THE CATHOLIC CHURCH, NO. 1415

To prepare for worthy reception of this sacrament, the faithful should observe the fast required in their Church. Bodily demeanor (gestures, clothing) ought to convey the respect, solemnity, and joy of this moment when Christ becomes our guest.

CATECHISM OF THE CATHOLIC CHURCH, NO. 1387

My wife and I are very fortunate to live in New Orleans, a predominately Catholic city, where among its many Catholic churches a weekly Mass can be found morning, noon, or night. Some of you may live in sections of the country where the opportunity to attend Mass during the week is limited. One suggestion is that you check with your parish priest or your diocesan office and ask for a daily Mass schedule. There also is a marvelous online resource to help you locate the time and place for Mass anywhere in the world: *www.masstimes.org*.

If you put forth the effort, the Holy Spirit, your Personal Trainer, just might provide you with the time and place to jog to Mass.

Visit the Blessed Sacrament

We have been speaking about receiving our spiritual nutrition by actually consuming Our Lord in the Eucharist. But there is another way of receiving spiritual nourishment: by simply being present before Him in the Blessed Sacrament.

QUOTE

Because Christ himself is present in the sacrament of the altar, he is to be honored with the worship of adoration. "To

visit the Blessed Sacrament is . . . a proof of gratitude, an
expression of love, and a duty of adoration toward Christ
our Lord" (Paul VI, *MF* 66).

CATECHISM OF THE CATHOLIC CHURCH, NO. 1418

I have also noticed that more and more people are jogging
to visit the Lord at adoration chapels. These adoration chapels
are springing up in parishes all over this nation, especially in the
New Orleans area. Quite a few are open 24/7.

It appears that those parishes that have made a commitment
to establish an adoration chapel have received tremendous blessings. Not only have these parishes seen attendance at Mass go
up, but participation by parishioners in other parish events has
increased as well. They have seen an increase in donations, too.
Most importantly, the spiritual fervor of these parishes has been
revitalized, along with the spiritual fervor of their priests.

I often hear magnificent testimonies from people who have
made a commitment to visit the Blessed Sacrament once a week
for an hour. I have talked to many people who for many years have
visited with the Lord in the middle of the night, and they say that
they wouldn't give this up for anything. In fact, they have told me
that they have been so spiritually nourished as a result of these
visits that their lives have been totally transformed.

My wife and I have not committed to a specific time each
week to visit the Blessed Sacrament, but we are often called by
the Holy Spirit (the Personal Trainer) to visit a particular adoration chapel. If you are unable to make a weekly commitment
to visit an adoration chapel, I strongly urge you to allow some
extra time, either before Mass or after Mass, to visit Jesus in
front of the tabernacle.

I also urge our priests to pray before the tabernacle before
saying Mass. Years ago, when I was an altar boy, I would arrive
at church to serve Mass and see the priest praying before the
tabernacle. This made a profound impression on me. Today,

when I go to church and *sometimes* see a priest at prayer before Mass, I am thankful for the wonderful example that he is setting for all of us.

Sacred Scripture

The Word of God also feeds us. Sacred Scripture is an integral part of living the Christian life!

QUOTE

"And such is the force and power of the Word of God that it can serve the Church as her support and vigor and the children of the Church as strength for their faith, food for the soul, and a pure and lasting font of spiritual life" (*DV* 21). Hence "access to Sacred Scriptures ought to be open wide to the Christian faithful" (*DV* 22).

CATECHISM OF THE CATHOLIC CHURCH, NO. 131

When I was growing up in the 1950s and '60s, the Catholic Church did not encourage people to read and study the Scriptures. Masses were celebrated in Latin, and reading the Bible was considered the privilege of clerics. Most Catholics acquired knowledge of the Scriptures through what was verbally presented by the priests in their homilies at church or occasionally by the religious sisters, brothers, or lay teachers at school.

My first real contact with the Bible came during my college years at Xavier University, in a course taught by Father Brugerman. In order to graduate from Xavier, students needed to complete 12 hours of theology, so I signed up for several Scripture classes. But, as I recall, most of these courses dealt more with the historical perspective of the Scriptures than the spiritual aspect. I must admit, though, sometimes I did enjoy the classes — whenever I could figure out what was going on!

The Second Vatican Council (1962-1965) brought about many liturgical changes and spiritual renewal among Catholics. The most noticeable change was that Mass would no longer be celebrated in Latin but instead in the vernacular — that is, the language commonly spoken by people. This change, as well as other changes brought about by the council, would have a dramatic effect on Catholics. A completely new avenue was opened for the laity to begin to read and study the Scriptures.

Although Vatican II has provided the Catholic laity with a wonderful opportunity to grow in their knowledge of the Scriptures and their faith, I personally believe that a vast majority of Catholics, especially men, still do not have a basic knowledge of the Scriptures or their faith.

On the other hand, it appears that our Protestant brothers have a vastly greater amount of knowledge of Scripture than do Catholics. On a more positive note, I have noticed in recent years more and more Catholics becoming interested in reading the Scriptures, participating in Bible study, and utilizing the *Catechism of the Catholic Church* as a study guide — all of which I highly recommend!

I was not really motivated to read the Scriptures until 1983, when I was introduced to a Bible-study course given by a group of people associated with the New Orleans Catholic Charismatic Renewal. This course really opened my eyes to a greater appreciation and understanding of the Scriptures. The spark was ignited by that Bible-study course, and the fire of the Holy Spirit has kindled my desire, over the years, to know and learn as much as possible about the Scriptures.

Scouting Report on the Scriptures
Let's spend some time highlighting the Church's teachings on the Scriptures. The *Catechism of the Catholic Church* (nos. 134-140) gives us a short review:

QUOTES

All Sacred Scripture is but one book, and this one book is Christ, "because all divine Scripture speaks of Christ, and all divine Scripture is fulfilled in Christ" (Hugh of St. Victor, *De arca Noe* 2, 8: PL 176, 642: cf. ibid. 2, 9: PL 176, 642-643).
CATECHISM OF THE CATHOLIC CHURCH, NO. 134

"The Sacred Scriptures contain the Word of God and, because they are inspired, they are truly the Word of God" (DV24).
CATECHISM OF THE CATHOLIC CHURCH, NO. 135

God is the author of Sacred Scripture because he inspired its human authors; he acts in them and by means of them. He thus gives assurance that their writings teach without error his saving truth (cf. *DV* 11).
CATECHISM OF THE CATHOLIC CHURCH, NO. 136

Interpretation of the inspired Scripture must be attentive above all to what God wants to reveal through the sacred authors for our salvation. What comes from the Spirit is not fully "understood except by the Spirit's action" (cf. Origen, *Hom. in Ex.* 4, 5: PG 12, 320).
CATECHISM OF THE CATHOLIC CHURCH, NO. 137

The Church accepts and venerates as inspired the 46 books of the Old Testament and the 27 books of the New.
CATECHISM OF THE CATHOLIC CHURCH, NO. 138

The four Gospels occupy a central place because Christ Jesus is their center.
CATECHISM OF THE CATHOLIC CHURCH, NO. 139

The unity of the two Testaments proceeds from the unity of God's plan and his Revelation. The Old Testament prepares

for the New and the New Testament fulfills the Old; the two
shed light on each other; both are the true Word of God.
                   CATECHISM OF THE CATHOLIC CHURCH, NO. 140

The Bible as a Playbook

For all of God's people, the Bible should become the "playbook" that leads us through our lives.

I mentioned earlier that many Catholics have a very limited grasp of their faith, and the main reason is their lack of
knowledge of the Scriptures. They just don't realize how much
they are missing by not pursuing a greater knowledge of the
Scriptures. I believe that a majority of the people in this group
are older, and that they have a basic fear of the Scriptures
because of their lack of exposure to these sacred writings during their younger days.

The younger generation has had much more exposure to the
Scriptures than older Catholics, because at Masses today the
Scripture readings are in the vernacular and of a wider variety
than in pre-Vatican II days. However, while younger Catholics
have had this greater exposure to the Scriptures, I am still not
convinced that our Catholic high schools and Catholic colleges
are teaching the Bible to the extent that it becomes engrained
in students' minds and, more importantly, in their hearts.

Sacred Scripture needs to be preached and taught in a way
that puts it within reach of its hearers. This is why Vatican II
teaches us that it is the responsibility of the bishops "to give the
faithful entrusted to them suitable instruction in the right use
of the divine books. . . . This can be done through translations
of the sacred texts, which are to be provided with the necessary
and really adequate explanations so that the children of the
Church may safely and profitably become conversant with the
Sacred Scriptures and be penetrated with their spirit" (Dog-
matic Constitution on Divine Revelation, no. 25).

Some Suggestions on How to Use Our Playbook (the Bible)

I would like to suggest to you several methods of adding scriptural nutrition to your life.

- Check with your parish office or ask your priest if there are any Bible-study courses you could attend.
- Catholics United for the Faith, publishers of the magazine *Lay Witness*, may be able to lead you to a good Scripture-study guide. (Catholics United for the Faith, 827 North Fourth St., Steubenville, OH 43952; phone 1-800-693-2484; website *www.cuf.org*.)
- Recently, a new group was established called National Resource Center for Catholic Men, and their purpose is to supply and support Catholic men by informing them of various resource materials. (National Resource Center for Catholic Men, P.O. Box 86381, Gaithersburg, MD 20886; phone 1-301-519-0646; website *www.catholicmensresources.org*.)

A Way to Get Started

Let me explain to you how I have come to have a greater appreciation and understanding of the Scriptures. Our Catholic Church is so wonderfully organized that every reading for every Sunday Mass for years to come has already been scheduled. In fact, every reading for every weekday Mass is also set. Before I attend Sunday Mass, I sit down with my wife and we read all of the readings.

After completing each reading, we use *The Navarre Bible* series (Scepter Publishers), with texts and commentaries, which gives a comprehensive explanation and insights into the various verses of the readings, all of which give us a better understanding of the sacred writings.

While attending Mass, we listen very attentively to the readings and pay close attention to the priest's homily, which usually focuses on one aspect of the readings.

Each week, by utilizing this process, we are able to come away from Mass thoroughly fed by the Word and with a greater understanding and appreciation of the readings. Consequently, we can apply whatever we have learned to the circumstances of our everyday life. My wife and I have been using this procedure for years, and it really has been a blessing and has nourished our souls spiritually. (We also try to review the readings before the weekday Masses. But I must admit that it has been difficult to also study the commentary, simply because of a lack of time.)

TIME OUT!

Reflect on the following points:

- Do you own a Bible? Is it a Catholic Bible?
- Ask the Holy Spirit (your Personal Trainer) to open your heart and mind, and then pick up the Bible and read it.
- What does the Lord have to say to you?
- Schedule some time every day to read the Bible, to be nourished by God's Word.

Some Helpful Resources

In addition to *The Navarre Bible* series, there are a number of good Bible commentaries to choose from. Your local Catholic bookstore may be able to help you in this regard. Purchase the one that you feel most comfortable with and which supplies you with the most information.

The readings for daily and Sunday Masses can be found easily by using a monthly publication called *Magnificat*, which is very handy and rather inexpensive (see page 68 for more information).

A Bible that I like to use for study purposes is *The Catholic Bible: Personal Study Edition* (Oxford University Press), which uses the New American Bible translation. The listing of the three-year cycle of readings (up through the year 2016) for Sunday Mass is located in the back.

The *Catechism* as the "Game Plan"

All Catholics, regardless of age, have a tremendous opportunity to nourish their faith by studying the *Catechism of the Catholic Church*, a resource that I have quoted throughout this book. Pope John Paul II has said that the *Catechism* is one of the highlights of his papacy.

I grew up in a time when the Catholic Church taught religion in a more structured manner, through the benefit of having so many priests and religious as instructors. One very effective and informative way they used to get their message across to us was the use of the Baltimore Catechism.

I will never forget some of the questions and answers that we had to memorize from this catechism. For instance: "Q. Who made the world? A. God made the world. Q. Why did God make you? A. God made me to know Him, to love Him, and to serve Him in this world, and to be happy with Him forever in heaven."

The Baltimore Catechism was an effective tool in its own way. However, the new *Catechism* provides contemporary Catholics with the entire game plan of our faith. This book is an incredible study guide that can be utilized for the rest of our lives, as something that we can continuously refer to concerning any issue pertaining to our faith. It also contains information regarding the teachings of the Catholic Church regarding morals and ethics. All of this wonderful information in the *Cat-*

echism is confirmed through the Scriptures and the teaching magisterium of the Church.

Some Possible Ways to Make Use of this Game Plan

Because the *Catechism of the Catholic Church* can be rather difficult to grasp at times, I would like to pass along several suggestions.

First of all, a group of us Catholic men in New Orleans "chipped in" and paid to have a young professor who teaches at the local seminary visit our prayer group over a period of weeks and give us a broad overview of the *Catechism* by sections. He would assign us a certain amount of readings to be completed before his seminar. He would then give his presentation of this section to our "class," followed by a question-and-answer period. This was a very effective way for us to get a basic understanding of the parts of the *Catechism* in a relatively short period of time.

You may want to check with your parish or diocese to see if any type of seminar on the *Catechism* is offered. If not, maybe you and your fellow parishioners could organize one, gather enough people to "fill the room," and then ask your priest or deacon to teach the course. The Prologue to the *Catechism* states that it is the obligation of the bishops first, and then of the priests, to educate the People of God (see no. 12).

There are two other books that I suggest you purchase in addition to the *Catechism*. The first one is *Introduction to the Catechism of the Catholic Church* (Ignatius Press), by Cardinal Joseph Ratzinger and Cardinal Christoph Schönborn. This book will instruct you on how to use the *Catechism*. The second work is *The Companion to the Catechism of the Catholic Church* (Ignatius Press), a compendium of texts that are referred to in the *Catechism*. This book allows you to easily locate various references that would otherwise take a tremendous amount of time and effort to research.

Finally, I recommend that you investigate a series of pamphlets on the *Catechism* that are published by St. Martin de Porres Lay Dominican Community. These pamphlets give short and concise teachings on various topics, such as the sacraments, which are contained in the *Catechism*. (For more information, write St. Martin de Porres Lay Dominican Community, New Hope, KY 40052; phone 1-800-789-9494.)

You may be thinking to yourself, "Boy, it takes plenty of reading and research to learn about our faith." You are exactly correct! It does take a lot of work. In order for someone to become a good teacher, carpenter, doctor, or athlete he must work at it. The more you work at something, the more proficient you become. So if you want to become a better Catholic, you must work at it.

In his apostolic letter introducing the *Catechism*, Pope John Paul II expresses his hope that "through the harmonious and complementary efforts of all the ranks of the People of God, may this *Catechism* be known and shared by everyone, so that the unity in faith whose supreme model and origin is found in the Unity of the Trinity may be strengthened and extended to the ends of the earth."

In closing this chapter on spiritual nutrition, I would like to confirm the Church's teaching on this concept of receiving dual spiritual nourishment through the Body of Christ and the Word of God:

QUOTE

The Church has always venerated the Scriptures as she venerates the Lord's Body. She never ceases to present to the faithful the bread of life, taken from the one table of God's Word and Christ's Body (cf. *DV* 21).

CATECHISM OF THE CATHOLIC CHURCH, NO. 103

ACTION PLAN

Things to Do

- Attend Mass (receive the Eucharist) at least one other time during the week besides Sunday. The ultimate goal is daily Mass.
- Read the Mass readings prior to attending Mass on Sunday.

Scripture: 1 Corinthians 11:26

For as often as you eat this bread and drink the cup, you proclaim the death of the Lord until he comes.

Rest in the Spirit

Noise and Activity

Our society seems unable to stand for anyone being quiet. Whenever people are faced with any extended period of quiet time, they become very jittery and anxious. It seems that our lives need to be constantly filled with activities and sounds.

If you look about and observe people, you will often see them talking on cell phones, whether they are waiting in air-port terminals, driving in their cars, walking down the street, sitting in restaurants, or jogging on a treadmill. You will even hear cell phones going off while attending church — and that totally drives me up a wall! When we are not talking on cell phones, we have a variety of other activities to occupy our time, such as watching television, listening to music on our headsets, reading the newspaper, playing video games, or simply surfing the net.

A recent poll showed that Americans spend incredible amounts of time watching television and reading newspapers. In fact, I have two friends who can hardly function without the television being on. One friend cannot go to sleep at night with-out the TV being on, and it usually stays on all night unless his wife turns it off. My other buddy turns the TV on immediately when he wakes up in the morning. I know this because I coached with this person, and we roomed next to each other in training camp. I would wake up in the morning, begin to stretch out in prayer, and all of a sudden I would hear the TV come on — and it would be rather loud! Because we were staying in col-lege dorms, the walls separating the rooms were very thin, and you could hear everything. Eventually, I had to ask him to please turn down his TV, or else I would have to move to another room. Of course, he graciously agreed.

Another problem that we face today is a workweek that goes beyond the traditional 40 hours. In many households, both spouses are working and are logging in some pretty hefty hours each day. By the time they arrive home after work and fighting traffic, they are exhausted, with not much time for rest, especially if they have children to attend to.

It seems that we are living in a time of much doubt, fear, and confusion, which has created much anxiety and stress in people's lives. Consequently, all of this anxiety and stress has caused people to become ill — physically, mentally, and spiritually.

People are searching for relief in all kinds of ways. Many of them are under the impression that if they fill their daily schedules with long work hours, as well as with all sorts of activities and sounds, then many of their problems will be alleviated. Eventually, they come to the conclusion that this is only a temporary solution.

Rest and Silence

There is nothing wrong with putting in a full day's work on the job or spending our leisure time on various activities and hobbies. However, I don't believe, in our fast-paced society, that we allow ourselves sufficient time for rest and silence so that we can reflect inwardly. Consequently, with all of this "commotion" going on in our personal lives, we really haven't left ourselves much time, if any, to rest in God's spirit and allow Him to speak to us.

Even God needed to take a day off to rest and reflect on His work after He had created the universe: "Thus the heavens and the earth and all their array were completed. Since on the seventh day God was finished with the work he had been doing, he *rested* on the seventh day from all the work he had undertaken. So God blessed the seventh day and made it holy, because on it he *rested* from all the work he had done in creation" (Genesis 2:1-3, emphasis added).

And what's more, God instructs us to do the same! In Exodus, God tells Moses that "Six days there are for doing work, but the seventh day is the sabbath of complete *rest*, sacred to the LORD" (Exodus 31:15, emphasis added).

The permanent solution to all of our problems and needs is to rest in the Lord. In order to rest in the Lord, we must train ourselves to be disciplined enough to carve out pockets of time from our busy schedules so that we can find the time to just be quiet and rest with Him. This is what Jesus tells us:

QUOTE

"Come to me, all you who labor and are burdened, and I will give you rest. Take my yoke upon you and learn from me, for I am meek and humble of heart; and you will find rest for yourselves. For my yoke is easy, and my burden light."

MATTHEW 11:28-29

How to Find Rest in the Lord

To me, the perfect image of resting in the Lord is depicted in the scene at the Last Supper, when John, the disciple that the Lord loved, laid his head on Jesus' chest. I don't think that Jesus told John to come over and lay his head on His chest because it would make a great picture. No, I think it was a gesture meant for each and every one of us, to let us know that He is always available for us to lay our heads on His chest and just rest.

The wonderful classic book *Abandonment to Divine Providence*, by Jean-Pierre de Caussade, tells us "that God knows all that is needed for the sanctification of every individual soul.

Holy Scripture contains one part and the workings of the Holy Spirit within the soul do the rest, using the particular ideal reserved for you. Now it is surely obvious that the only way to receive the impress of this idea is to put oneself quietly in the hands of God and that none of our own efforts and mental striving can be of any use at all."

Since we are not accustomed to this type of quiet time, we must pray to God and ask Him to provide us with sufficient graces to be still, so that we can rest in His spirit.

The best time for resting in the Lord is usually during our prayer time. I suggest that you start your practice of resting in the spirit during your weekend prayer time because you will have a little extra time and maybe you will not be as rushed as you would be during the week.

How does one do this?

- First, begin this quieting process by finding a very comfortable place to position your body.
- Next, take several deep breaths to calm yourself, and then begin a very systematic breathing pattern.
- Once your body has begun to relax, focus all of your attention on quieting your mind. (This is very difficult because the devil tries to intervene by filling our minds with different thoughts, temptations, and distractions. Satan will do anything to prevent us from communicating with Jesus.)
- Call upon your Personal Trainer, the Holy Spirit, to clear your mind of anything that is not of Him, and to fill your heart with His Spirit. (Again, this will not be easy because the devil doesn't give up without putting up a good fight.)
- Persevere and hang in there. Eventually, you will experience a total resting in the Lord, and you will hear His voice in your heart.

As Jeremiah the prophet wrote: "Give ear, listen humbly, / for the LORD speaks" (Jeremiah 13:15).

How Will God Speak to You?

Do not become discouraged if you are having a hard time quieting yourself or if it doesn't seem as though the Lord is speaking to you. Keep on! Just remember that we are used to constantly *talking* and asking the Lord for this and that — and often we don't even realize that we're doing it. Even though we might not be saying things aloud, we are constantly bouncing thoughts around in our mind. But God is so gentle and polite that He will not interrupt us when we are speaking.

I remember becoming frustrated during my prayer time because I could not hear the Lord speaking to my heart. One day I finally realized that it was pretty difficult for the Lord to answer me when I was talking continuously. He could not get a word in edgewise!

If you are waiting for God to speak to you directly in a loud, clear voice, you might have a long wait. Throughout salvation history, God has spoken directly to someone very seldom. He did so on one occasion when He spoke to Moses out of a burning bush (Exodus 3:2-4:17). God certainly has a sense of humor, but normally He doesn't speak to us in such a dramatic way as a burning bush. Rather, He speaks to us in ways we are somewhat familiar with. Here are some examples of the various ways that God may choose to speak to us:

- **Through His Word:** He may place in our mind a particular Scripture passage that touches our heart.
- **Through another person:** He may give another person a "word" that is really meant for us. And this word may be a solution to a problem that we have been dealing with.
- **Through a "gut" feeling:** While we are discerning about something, God may allow us to experience a feeling in

the middle of our stomach that makes us feel comfortable about a decision we are about to make.

- **Through a vision:** While we are praying, the Lord may allow us to experience a vision that will be helpful to us, so that, for example, we will have a better understanding of a relationship we are struggling with.

Also, we must realize that God will speak to us in *His* time frame, not ours, and according to *His* plan, not ours. We might not like it, but the answer to our prayer quite possibly could be "No." He knows what is best for us.

TIME OUT!

Now that we have gone over the "hows," let's take a moment to practice:

- Spend a few moments resting in the Lord. What happens?

Personal Experiences

Let me share with you two personal experiences when God spoke to me during this time of resting in the spirit.

The first experience occurred when I was coaching special teams for the Chicago Bears under Coach Dave Wannstedt. I was in my fourth year, and it was time to sign a new contract. The Bears had just offered me a two-year contract, but something inside me told me not to sign the contract. I shared this with my wife, and I asked her if she would begin to pray with me about this situation. So we began to pray on a daily basis.

Several weeks had gone by, and Coach Wannstedt was pressing me for an answer. I told him that I had not yet made up my mind. He replied that he couldn't wait much longer. If I couldn't give him an answer within the next several days, he said, then he would be forced to go in another direction and hire someone else. I told him that I completely understood his position, and I thanked him for the extra time for me to make a decision.

I mentioned to him that I was praying about the situation. Dave understood my position because he is a very devout Catholic. In fact, he and I had attended a Bible-study class together. But the fact remained that he had to make a coaching decision concerning my position, and time was running out.

One day while my wife and I were praying, the answer came to me. I had a gut feeling that God wanted me to move on from the Bears. My wife had a similar feeling. So I went to Coach Wannstedt and told him of my decision, and he wished me good luck. Before I left his office, he asked me if I had another job offer and I told him that I did not. I know he probably thought I was crazy, because two-year contracts for assistants in the NFL back then didn't come easily.

My wife and I continued to pray and ask our Personal Trainer, the Holy Spirit, for His direction for our future in the coaching business. The very next day during our prayer time, my wife received this Scripture passage from the Lord: "But the LORD sent a large fish, that swallowed Jonah; and he remained in the belly of the fish three days and three nights" (Jonah 2:1).

I said to my wife that I thought something might happen within the next three days. A couple of days went by, and nothing happened. But we continued to pray and *wait* for the Lord.

On the evening of the third day, I went to the adoration chapel at Marytown. While I was gone, my wife received a phone call from Coach Mike Ditka, returning our earlier call. I had called Coach Ditka to let him know that I had resigned from the Bears; I didn't want him to find out from the news media. He was the person who had initially hired me in Chicago, and I called him out of respect. My wife began to explain to him that I had resigned, and that we wanted him to know firsthand.

Coach Ditka interrupted her and said, "Don't worry about a thing. I've just accepted the head coaching position for the New Orleans Saints, and I want Danny to be my offensive coordinator." He told her to keep this in strict confidence because it hadn't been released to the news media yet. When I got home and heard what Coach Ditka had said, I almost fell over. My wife and I began thanking God for answering our prayers.

Sometimes when the Lord answers a particular prayer, it is quite interesting to eventually find out that the first answer might not be the final one. Even though God had answered my prayers — I was going back to New Orleans as Coach Ditka's new offensive coordinator, and the fans were excited because of their hopes that we would take the Saints back to the playoffs — the next three years were anything but glorious times. Things got worse before they got better, and after three years the entire coaching staff was fired. The one positive thing that came out of this situation was that I had one year remaining on my contract.

My wife and I turned to prayer about this situation and asked our Personal Trainer, the Holy Spirit, to guide us once again. To make a long story short, over a period of time I received several job offers to remain in NFL coaching. I also received an offer from a friend of mine to be a partner in a very successful business of his. Almost simultaneously, Joe Canizaro, another prominent businessman who happened to be a longtime friend, called and invited me to go to lunch.

During this luncheon, we talked about my future. I informed Joe that I really didn't have any set plans, but that I was leaving it in God's hands. As we were about to finish our meal, out of the clear blue sky he said to me, "Why don't you come and run our family foundation." He caught me off guard. I replied, "I have never done anything like that, but let me have some time to think about it and pray about it."

With these offers in hand, all kinds of things started flashing through my mind. Did I really want to continue coaching?

The money and the fame in the National Football League were alluring. The idea of running a portion of a business was attractive, but it left me feeling a little restless. Operating a family foundation was something that was intriguing but also something that I didn't know anything about.

I know that most of you men reading this book probably would say, "If I had this decision to make, it would be a no-brainer! I would stay in the NFL and coach." And you businessmen would probably say, "What a great opportunity to own a piece of a successful business!"

Well, after several weeks of prayer and discernment, the final decision came from my *gut* and not from my head. Financially, either the NFL or the business proposition was the best way to go, but I felt that God was calling me to a new challenge in life. So I accepted the position as the executive director of the Donum Dei Foundation. (For those who are curious, the Latin phrase *donum Dei* means "gift of God.")

These two stories are perfect examples of how God was leading my wife and me on a path that was set forth by Him long ago. All we had to do was pray and rest in His spirit, listen, trust, and follow the directions of our Personal Trainer, the Holy Spirit.

God's Ways Are Not Our Ways

QUOTE

For I know well the plans I have in mind for you, says the LORD, plans for your welfare, not for woe! plans to give you a future full of hope. When you call me, when you go to pray to me, I will listen to you. When you look for me, you will find me. Yes, when you seek me with all your heart, you will find me with you, says the LORD, and I will change your lot.

JEREMIAH 29:11-14

The Lord has changed my lot, and He has allowed me to experience inwardly His joy and peace through the wonderful gifts we are able to provide to people through the Donum Dei Foundation.

We must be patient and *wait* for the Lord. We must remember that He knows and will provide what we *need*, not what we want; and that He will answer our prayers in *His* time frame, not ours.

The psalmist speaks so beautifully to this when he writes: "Trust in the LORD and do good / that you may dwell in the land and live secure. / Find your delight in the LORD / who will give you your heart's desire. / Commit your way to the LORD; / trust that God will act" (Psalm 37:3-5). And finally, he says this: "Be still before the LORD; / wait for God" (Psalm 37:7).

In closing, I want to share this beautiful passage about how God spoke to Elijah on Mount Horeb. I think this will best explain the necessity for us to be quiet and wait for the Lord so that we can hear Him:

QUOTE

Then the LORD said, "Go outside and stand on the mountain before the LORD; the LORD will be passing by." A strong and heavy wind was rending the mountains and crushing rocks before the LORD — but the LORD was not in the wind. After the wind there was an earthquake — but the LORD was not in the earthquake. After the earthquake there was fire — but the LORD was not in the fire. After the fire there was a tiny whispering sound. When he heard this, Elijah hid his face in his cloak and went and stood at the entrance of the cave. A voice said to him, "Elijah, why are you here?"

1 KINGS 19:11-13

ACTION PLAN

Things to Do

- Go to an adoration chapel at least once a week — and just rest in the Lord.

Scripture: Psalm 62:2

My soul rests in God alone, / from whom comes my salvation.

Make an Action Plan

To Be Holy

We must realize that God wants us to strive to be holy as He is holy. This may come as quite a shock, that God wants us to be like Him. How can we — who are, after all, created beings — be like Almighty God? Quite simply, to be holy means that we are "set apart for God," and that He is our No. 1 priority.

Sacred Scripture reminds us about this call to holiness many times, in particular in these inspiring verses:

QUOTES

God created man in his image; / in the divine image he created him; / male and female he created them.

GENESIS 1:27

"For I, the LORD, am your God; and you shall make and keep yourselves holy, because I am holy."

LEVITICUS 11:44

Strive for peace with everyone, and for that holiness without which no one will see the Lord.

HEBREWS 12:14

But, as he who called you is holy, be holy yourselves in every aspect of your conduct, for it is written, "Be holy because I [am] holy."

1 PETER 1:15-16

At this point, many of you might be saying to yourselves, "Wow! This is an awfully large task. How can I ever live up to this set of standards?" I must admit that the first time I read those particular words of Scripture, I thought the very same thing. But after giving it much thought and prayer, I came to the realization that God wants us to try to do our best, because He will be with us every step of the way.

QUOTE

[A Christian] needs to be not only linked to Jesus Christ but to adhere to Him, to be firmly attached to Him: to be separated from Him to the least degree is to be lost. . . . Notice all the comparisons the apostle [Paul] makes to explain this intimate unity: Jesus Christ is the head, we the body, for there can be no gap between head and body. He is the foundation, we the building; He is the vine, we the branches; He is the spouse, we the bride; He is the shepherd, we the flock; He is the way alone which we are to travel; we are the temple, and God dwells therein; He is the firstborn, we His brethren; He is the heir, we co-heirs; He is life and we have life through Him; He is the resurrection and we men are raised up; He is the light by which darkness is dispelled.

ST. JOHN CHRYSOSTOM, *HOMILY ON 1 CORINTHIANS*

The *Catechism of the Catholic Church* states, " 'All Christians in any state or walk of life are called to the fullness of Christian life and to the perfection of charity' (*LG* 40, paragraph 2)" (no. 2013). *All* are called to holiness! As Jesus instructed His followers, "Be perfect, just as your heavenly Father is perfect" (Matthew 5:48).

Evaluate Your Progress

Every year, before the beginning of the new NFL season, the coaching staffs of each team meet to discuss goals for the offensive, defensive, and special teams for the upcoming season. Once these goals have been established, the staff presents them to the players, and then the goals are posted in the locker room for everyone to view on a daily basis.

Periodically, during the season, the coaches will review the goals with the players, to see if everything is on schedule. During my years in the NFL, both as a player and as a coach, I have observed that having these goals written down puts more pressure on individuals as well as the team as a whole to commit themselves to the success of these goals.

This is why I think it is necessary for all of us to write down our goals for our spiritual life, so that (1) we can review them on a periodic basis and (2) be more committed to reaching them.

Goals

Let me begin this goal-setting process with you by recommending some initial goals in the areas that we have already discussed earlier concerning our spiritual fitness workout.

I. Get the Holy Spirit as your Personal Trainer.
   • Consult with your Personal Trainer at the start of every day and throughout the day.
II. Scout the enemies of your spiritual life.
   • Know your enemy and be prepared for the battle! Remember that working out spiritually is a battle (much in the same way that a physical workout is a battle for most people).
III. Stretch out in prayer.
   • Commit to prayer by setting aside 15 minutes every day. If you have already started stretching out in

prayer, increase the amount of time so that eventually you will be spending 45 to 60 minutes each day in prayer.

IV. Run away from temptation.

- Examine your conscience, and determine what is the devil's No. 1 tactic to tempt you to sin. It could be pornography or booze (as the latter was in my case). Whatever it is, strive to avoid it at all costs, and ask your Personal Trainer (the Holy Spirit) to supply you with the strength and grace to overcome this temptation.

V. Lift up others in prayer.

- Make an effort each day to convince yourself that you will live (that day) with a positive attitude when dealing with people and that you will pray for them.

VI. Receive your spiritual nutrition.

- Make an effort to attend Mass as often as possible each week, striving to build up to daily Mass.
- Begin a study program that incorporates the Scriptures and the *Catechism of the Catholic Church*.

VII. Rest in the spirit.

- Whenever possible, try to quiet yourself inwardly so that you can hear God. As I mentioned earlier in the book, a good time and place to rest in the Lord is during a visit to an adoration chapel. If one is available, stop by the chapel for a weekly visit.

VIII. Make an action plan.

- Create a plan, and stick to it!

I have designed a format for myself that I would like to share with you, to make it easier for you to write down your commitments to the Lord. As you already know, I believe that it is important for us to write things down, to check our progress every so often. By the way, this action plan should be *very private*, something between you and God.

When we make our commitments to God, it is not easy to back out when things get difficult or do not go our way. So, when filling out this sheet, do not overcommit yourself to a whole list of things. Think in terms of the acronym SAM: Specific, Attainable, Measurable.

Choose things that are specific, things that are realistic for you to do, and things that you can evaluate or measure, to determine your progress. Keep it simple at first, and then add new workout exercises as you see development and strength in your program. Build confidence with your "friend" SAM.

Let me share with you some of the commitments that I have made to the Lord in my Individual Spiritual Fitness Action Plan. You may use this sample format on the following page, or you may design something else, whichever is more comfortable for you and suits your purposes. Read this over now.

Since I have presented you with some of the things that I have committed to the Lord, now I want to provide you with your own Individual Spiritual Fitness Action Plan sheet (see page 145) so that you can jot down some of the things that you are going to personally commit to the Lord.

Pray and ask God to put on your heart a few things that will get you started. Once you feel comfortable with your Individual Spiritual Fitness Action Plan, you can always add a few new things. You should go before the Lord in prayer once every quarter (once every three months) to evaluate your progress.

A Time of Blessing

Pope John Paul II has said that we are experiencing a "new springtime" in our Church.

Regardless of the negative attitude that some people have toward the Church, especially in the news media, I believe this

INDIVIDUAL SPIRITUAL FITNESS ACTION PLAN

A Catholic Man in Action
(Sample)

I, Danny Abramowicz, commit the following to the Lord for the next three months:

1. To enlist the help of my Personal Trainer, the Holy Spirit
   a. Every morning
   b. Throughout the day
   c. Enlist a spiritual director

2. To produce a scouting report
   a. Examine my conscience every day

3. To stretch out in prayer
   a. 45 minutes each morning

4. To run away from temptation and from sin
   a. Receive the Sacrament of Reconciliation once a month

5. To lift up others in prayer
   a. Tell my wife and children how much I love and appreciate them
   b. Tell every priest I meet that I appreciate him

6. To receive spiritual nutrition
   a. Read daily readings before attending Mass
   b. Attend daily Mass and receive the Eucharist

7. To rest in the spirit
   a. Try to rest in the Lord during part of my prayer time

Danny Abramowicz

Danny Abramowicz

COACHING POINTS
1. Review personally each week
2. Review before the Lord at the end of the quarter
3. Discuss with spiritual director (monthly)

INDIVIDUAL SPIRITUAL FITNESS ACTION PLAN

A Catholic Man in Action
(My Plan)

I, _____, commit the following to the Lord for the next three months:

1. To enlist the help of my Personal Trainer, the Holy Spirit
   a. _____
   b. _____
   c. _____

2. To produce a scouting report
   a. _____

3. To stretch out in prayer
   a. _____

4. To run away from temptation and from sin
   a. _____

5. To lift up others in prayer
   a. _____
   b. _____

6. To receive spiritual nutrition
   a. _____
   b. _____

7. To rest in the spirit
   a. _____

_____
(Your Name)

COACHING POINTS
1. Review personally each week
2. Review before the Lord at the end of the quarter
3. Discuss with spiritual director (monthly)

will be a time of blessings for the Church and all of God's people.

Why don't you take this advice from an old "has-been" former Saint (New Orleans, that is) and allow your Personal Trainer, the Holy Spirit, to begin training you spiritually so that, through the grace of God, you can receive the benefits of these workouts, which are the gifts and the fruits of His Spirit?

QUOTES

[Regarding the gifts:] The Spirit of the LORD shall rest upon him: / a spirit of wisdom and of understanding, / A spirit of counsel and of strength, / a spirit of knowledge and of fear of the LORD.

ISAIAH 11:2; also see the CATECHISM OF THE
CATHOLIC CHURCH, NOS. 1830-1831

[Regarding the fruits:] The fruit of the Spirit is love, joy, peace, patience, kindness, generosity, faithfulness, gentleness, self-control.

GALATIANS 5:22-23; also see the
CATECHISM OF THE CATHOLIC CHURCH, NO. 1832

Team Work

A great deal of our attention has been focused on our own Individual Spiritual Fitness Action Plan. Now I would like to share with you the benefit of being part of a "group," or "team," spiritual fitness workout plan.

At times, it becomes very difficult to continue alone with our individual workout plan. It seems as though people may look at us differently and consider us odd, or maybe even weak, because we have a personal relationship with Jesus, along with a daily prayer life that includes attendance at Mass several times a week. One begins to feel alone, as if on some island with no one to talk to about spiritual matters.

As a follow-up to the Individual Spiritual Fitness Action Plan, I strongly urge men to think about joining a small men's prayer group. These team gatherings will open men's eyes to the fact that it is important for brothers to gather, in order to support, encourage, and hold one another accountable to a Christian model of manhood.

The most successful small-group meeting program for men was started approximately 10 years ago in Cincinnati by Kevin Lynch and a group of other faithful Catholic men. The Catholic Men's Fellowship has grown over the years, and today there are groups in approximately 175 parishes throughout metropolitan Cincinnati. These men's groups have flourished for three reasons.

First, Kevin and his men have been obedient to God and have worked very hard to evangelize other men.

Second, the Archdiocese of Cincinnati and the Diocese of Covington have been very supportive of the fellowship and have helped it grow. Three years ago, I spoke at their annual men's conference, and when it came time to hear confessions, there were more than 100 priests administering the Sacrament of Reconciliation. Archbishop Daniel Pilarczyk of Cincinnati and Bishop Robert Muench of Covington (now bishop of Baton Rouge) concelebrated the Mass at the conference. These bishops and priests did not just *talk* to the men about attending the conference, but they also *participated* in it. Consequently, the men responded to their example by also participating, and as a result they were touched spiritually.

Third, it is obvious that the Holy Spirit (our Personal Trainer) has been leading and directing Kevin and his group of men, and I believe He is calling all men back to a spiritual awakening.

The Holy Spirit Is Calling Men

Let me expand upon something I spoke about earlier in the book, just to give you an example of how I sense that the Holy Spirit has His hand in this call to men to return to a life of spiritual fitness.

In 1985, the Holy Spirit put on my heart the idea to begin a small Catholic men's group at my home. At first, I thought this was just my imagination. But the idea persisted, especially during prayer time. So I decided that I should act on this prompting. If it was of God, it would probably work; and if it was not, it would fail.

I began by calling 12 men whose names sort of popped into my head. Some of them I knew well, while the others I had met just casually. I told them that the Lord put on my heart the idea to start a prayer group at my house, and that I was calling them to see if they were interested. Well, an amazing thing happened! All 12 men said they were interested, and all of them showed up at my house for the first meeting. Anybody in advertising or marketing will tell you that a 40 or 50 percent response rate to a sales promotion is terrific, but to receive 100 percent response is phenomenal. After that first meeting, I was convinced that something special was about to happen.

Because none of us had ever led a prayer meeting, and most of us had not even attended one, all we did for the first four or five meetings was pray and praise the Lord. News of the meetings began to spread by word of mouth, and men started to show up at my house every first and third Monday night of the month. Most of these men I had never seen before in my life. Attendance at the meetings grew — so much so, in fact, that we eventually had to rearrange the furniture in our house. My wife didn't mind, though, because she also sensed that something very special was taking place.

The basic format up to this point was focused on prayer, worship, and the Scriptures. After about six months, men began to stand up during the prayer meetings and *share* very personal things in their lives. This kind of sharing spurred other men to talk about things going on in their lives. All of us who had been involved from the beginning knew that the Holy Spirit was moving upon the hearts of the men in the Monday Night Disciples prayer group.

Eventually, the men volunteered to bring snacks, sandwiches, and soft drinks, and my wife agreed to bake pastries. We invited the men to remain after the meeting to enjoy some fellowship. This Team Spiritual Fitness Workout remained at my house for three years. Finally, it grew in size to where we were averaging about 90 men a meeting. It was incredible! But it was time to move. Fortunately, we had several priests who were part of the group. One of them, Father Bernie O'Brien, offered us his place, and so we moved to St. Frances Cabrini Parish.

The Monday Night Disciples are still flourishing to this day, with several groups meeting in the metropolitan New Orleans area. I have no doubt, in my mind or heart, that the Holy Spirit has kept and will keep this group alive. We are a group of men who recognize that we are sinners, but we are always faithful to our God by lifting Him up in prayer, worship, and reflecting on His Word.

After experiencing the power of the Holy Spirit in building up the Catholic Men's Fellowship and the Monday Night Disciples, I am certain that the Holy Spirit will use that same power to touch men's hearts all over this world, encouraging them to either start or join a small spiritual fitness group.

I don't recommend starting the *individual* and the *team* spiritual fitness workouts simultaneously. First of all, you should begin with your individual plan. Then, once you feel comfortable with that, you may want to check with other men in your parish and see if any small groups have been established. Or you may ask some of your friends if they are interested in starting up a small group, either in a home or at the parish.

On the following pages, I will present an outline of the Team Spiritual Fitness Workout, which will include:

1. A mission statement.
2. The purpose of the team workout.
3. The strategy of the team workout.
4. A step-by-step procedure on how to start a small group in your parish or home.
5. A Team Spiritual Fitness Action Plan (sample).

The Monday Night Disciples have used this structure for 17 years, and I offer it to you for your consideration and use. Of course, this is simply an example to help you get started.

TEAM SPIRITUAL FITNESS WORKOUT

Mission Statement

To *strengthen ourselves inwardly* through these spiritual fitness workouts so that we become godly men who can make a difference in our homes, parishes, workplaces, and communities.

Purpose of Workout

1. To bring men together to stretch out in *prayer* and *worship*.
2. To allow the *Word of God* to penetrate into each of our hearts.
3. To *educate* ourselves and others through the Lord's teachings found in the *Scriptures* and the *Catechism*.
4. To *share* with other men how God works in each of our lives on a daily basis.
5. To *recruit* other men to participate in these spiritual workouts.

Strategy

1. *Stretch out* in prayers of forgiveness and thanksgiving.
2. *Warm up* with songs of praise and worship.
3. *Breathe in* the Word of God.
4. *Teamwork* — Encourage one another through sharing ourselves.
5. *Growth* through spiritual nutrition — the Lord's teachings found in the Scriptures and the *Catechism*.
6. *Lift up* and fortify others through prayers of petition and healing.
7. *Huddle* for fellowship and refreshments.
8. *Recruit* new team members.

Getting Started

Step I — Leadership

A. Begin with a core group, with three or more men gathered in prayer for guidance from the Holy Spirit.
B. Choose two men to be initial captains.
C. As you grow, encourage others to get more involved. The size of groups can vary: 5-10, 15-20, or 25-30.
D. Decide on a music leader. Having a person who plays a guitar is very important. Music sets the spiritual tone of the workouts.

Step II — Approval

A. Set up an appointment with the pastor. You want his approval, but also ask him to join you in the workouts. Assure him that this is not another thing added to his "plate" of responsibilities.
B. Make sure that you invite any deacons, if they are not already involved.
C. Make sure that you understand the mission of the spiritual fitness workout before meeting with the pastor.

D. Be prepared to explain to the pastor the spiritual fitness workout program. Priests need men, and men need priests.

Step III — Fitness Workout Centers

A. *Parish* — Choose an area in the parish center or in the church that has some privacy and gives you the room to expand.

B. *Homes* — These are very nice. But your choices will be limited by the size of your group — and that's okay.

C. *Workplaces* — Small groups of five or six can meet at someone's office for a breakfast or lunch meeting (once or twice a month).

Step IV — Workout Dates

A. Schedule meetings for twice a month. (Examples: first and third Thursdays, 7:30-9:00 pm.; or second and fourth Saturdays, 7:00-8:30 a.m.)

B. Saturday mornings usually are good times for dads with young children.

Step V — How to Promote Workouts

A. Make it known that all men are welcomed.

B. Contact the parish secretary to place a notice in the parish bulletin. This can be very helpful.

C. Get permission to make announcements at Mass.

D. Spread the word by word of mouth, which seems to work the best and is the most personal.

E. Make phone calls. You will need to make extra ones in the beginning.

Step VI — Equipment

A. *Men's Team Spiritual Fitness Workout program outline and action plan* — These will help you direct the entire workout.

B. *Bible* — **This is your "playbook."**

C. *Catechism of the Catholic Church* — **This is your "game plan."**

D. *Music sheet to use for songs of worship and praise* — An overhead projector works great. There's no need for songbooks.

E. *Cassette/CD player* — Use one if you are unable to find a person to lead with a guitar.

Step VII — Responsibilities

A. Find several men who are willing to take turns opening and closing the meeting rooms.

B. Sometimes refreshments are supplied by the parish. But more than likely, an offering should be collected to purchase soft drinks, coffee, and cookies.

C. Everyone makes sure that the room is put back in order.

Step VIII — Growth

A. Try to follow up with a phone call to each new member that you bring to the workout. Make sure everything is okay with him, and remind him of the next workout.

B. Each member should invite one new man every month. Follow through by encouraging him and personally inviting him to keep coming back.

PLEASE NOTE: The National Resource Center for Catholic Men has plenty of materials to help you get started. You can contact them online at *www.catholicmensresources.org*. Now turn to the next two pages for the sample Team Spiritual Fitness Action Plan.

TEAM SPIRITUAL FITNESS ACTION PLAN

Catholic Men in Action
(Sample)

**Workouts: 7:30-9:00 p.m.,
first and third Mondays of the month**

Greeting — Welcome everyone and introduce all new people.

I. Stretch-out Prayer: Have someone lead a prayer that consists of:
   A. *Forgiveness* — Ask God the Father to forgive our sins, to wash us clean.
   B. *Surrender to Jesus* — Turn over to Him all cares, worries, and anxieties. We empty ourselves.
   C. *The Holy Spirit* (Personal Trainer) — Let Him direct us in building up the main muscle, "the heart."

II. Warm-up/Breathing (approximately 25 minutes): *Praise* and *worship* through song. Music helps us reach a high praise level to honor our God.
   A. *Joyful songs* (3) — After we finish, allow a few minutes of quiet, to rest in the spirit. Listen to the Lord speak to us. Someone could receive a Scripture passage or word from the Lord at this time.
   B. *Several more songs* — These should be of slow tempo, to quiet us down and wait on the Lord. Breathe in the Word of God. Read from the Scriptures.
   C. *More songs of high reverent worship* — We praise and worship with a contrite heart. We will exhale His love.

III. Team Work (approximately 40 minutes): This is growth through spiritual nutrition. During this time, we have the following options:

    A. *The Catechism* ("game plan") — Study such topics as the sacraments, grace, Mary, or the papacy.
    B. *The Scriptures* ("playbook") — Give a chalk talk on a particular passage.
    C. *Sharing Time* — We encourage one another by sharing ourselves, giving testimony and witness on how God's power has changed our lives.

IV. Lifting (10 minutes): Lift up and fortify others through prayers of petition and prayers for healing (physically, mentally, and especially spiritually).

Closing
    • *Announcements*
    • *Closing song: "Our God Reigns"*

V. Huddle (15 minutes): This is the time for fellowship and refreshments, to enjoy one another's company.

VI.Recruit (ongoing): Bring in new team members.

Appendix

Kicking off Your Prayer Time

I believe that it is essential to begin every prayer period with the two most fundamental and powerful prayers of the Church: the Apostles' Creed and the Our Father. Even though we have heard and recited these prayers many times over the years, let's try to take the time to prayerfully meditate on each word of these inspired texts when we pray them.

Apostles' Creed

St. Ambrose tells us, "This creed is the spiritual seal, our heart's meditation, and an ever-present guardian; it is, unquestionably, the treasure of our souls." In case you have forgotten the words to the Apostles' Creed, here they are:

> I believe in God, the Father almighty, creator of heaven and earth. I believe in Jesus Christ, his only Son, our Lord. He was conceived by the power of the Holy Spirit and born of the Virgin Mary. He suffered under Pontius Pilate, was crucified, died, and was buried. He descended to the dead. On the third day he rose again. He ascended into heaven, and is seated at the right hand of the Father. He will come again to judge the living and the dead. I believe in the Holy Spirit, the holy catholic Church, the communion of saints, the forgiveness of sins, the resurrection of the body, and the life everlasting. Amen.

Our Father (Lord's Prayer)

St. Thomas Aquinas said: "The Lord's Prayer is the most perfect of prayers. . . . In it, we ask not only for all the things we can rightly desire but also in the sequence that they should be desired. This prayer not only teaches us to ask for things, but also in what order we should desire them."

The great St. Augustine remarked: "Run through all the words of the holy prayers [in Scripture], and I do not think that you will find anything in them that is not contained and included in the Lord's Prayer." Again, in case you have forgotten the words to the Our Father, here they are:

Our Father, who art in heaven, hallowed be thy name; thy kingdom come; thy will be done on earth as it is in heaven. Give us this day our daily bread; and forgive us our trespasses as we forgive those who trespass against us; and lead us not into temptation, but deliver us from evil. Amen.

Ask your Personal Trainer, the Holy Spirit, to make the words of these prayers come alive for you in your time of reflection. I can assure you, with His help and your perseverance, these two prayers will speak to your heart like never before.

Other Prayers

Here are some other common prayers that you may need to re-memorize if you've been away for a while.

Sign of the Cross

In the name of the Father, and of the Son, and of the Holy Spirit. Amen.

Glory Be
Glory be to the Father, and to the Son, and to the Holy Spirit. As it was in the beginning, is now, and ever shall be, world without end. Amen.

Invocation of the Holy Spirit
Come, Holy Spirit, fill the hearts of your faithful, and kindle in them the fire of your love. Send forth your Spirit, and they shall be created. And you shall renew the face of the earth.

O God, who by the light of the Holy Spirit did instruct the hearts of the faithful, grant by the same Holy Spirit we may be truly wise and ever rejoice in his consolation. We ask this through Christ our Lord. Amen.

Marian Prayers

Hail Mary
Hail, Mary, full of grace. The Lord is with thee. Blessed art thou among women, and blessed is the fruit of thy womb, Jesus. Holy Mary, Mother of God, pray for us sinners, now and at the hour of our death. Amen.

Memorare
Remember, O most gracious Virgin Mary, that never was it known that anyone who fled to your protection, implored your help, or sought your intercession was left unaided. Inspired by this confidence, I fly unto you, O virgin of virgins, my Mother. To you do I come, before you I stand, sinful and sorrowful. O Mother of the

Word Incarnate, despise not my petitions, but in your mercy, hear and answer me. Amen.

The Rosary

(From *Praying the Rosary: With the Joyful, Luminous, Sorrowful, and Glorious Mysteries*, by Michael Dubruiel and Amy Welborn.)

Mysteries of the Rosary

The Joyful Mysteries (prayed on Mondays and Saturdays)
> The Annunciation to Mary
> The Visitation of Mary
> The Nativity of Our Lord
> The Presentation of the Lord
> The Finding in the Temple

The Luminous Mysteries (prayers on Thursdays)
> The Baptism of the Lord
> The Wedding Feast at Cana
> The Preaching of the Kingdom of God
> The Transfiguration of the Lord
> The Institution of the Eucharist

The Sorrowful Mysteries (prayed on Tuesdays and Fridays)
> The Agony in the Garden
> The Scourging at the Pillar
> The Crowning With Thorns
> The Carrying of the Cross
> The Crucifixion of Our Lord

The Glorious Mysteries (prayed on Wednesdays and Sundays)

The Resurrection of Our Lord
The Ascension of Our Lord
The Descent of the Holy Spirit
The Assumption of the Blessed Virgin
The Coronation of Mary as Queen of Heaven

Rosary Prayers

Fátima Prayer
O my Jesus, forgive us our sins, save us from the fires of hell, lead all souls to heaven, especially those who have most need of your mercy. Amen.

Hail, Holy Queen
Hail, Holy Queen, Mother of Mercy, our life, our sweetness, and our hope. To thee do we cry, poor banished children of Eve; to thee do we send up our sighs, mourning, and weeping in this valley of tears. Turn then, most gracious advocate, thine eyes of mercy toward us, and after this, our exile, show unto us the blessed fruit of thy womb, Jesus. O clement, O loving, O sweet Virgin Mary.

V. Pray for us, O Holy Mother of God.
R. That we may be made worthy of the promises of Christ.

Concluding Rosary Prayer
Let us pray: O God, whose only begotten Son, by his life, death, and resurrection, has purchased for us the rewards of eternal life, grant, we beseech thee, that meditating upon these mysteries of the Most Holy Rosary

of the Blessed Virgin Mary, we may imitate what they contain and obtain what they promise, through the same Christ our Lord. Amen.

Preparing for Confession

Ten Commandments
(From *Catholic Family Prayer Book*, by Jacquelyn Lindsey.)

1. I, the Lord, am your God. You shall not have other gods besides me.
2. You shall not take the name of the Lord, your God, in vain.
3. Remember to keep holy the Sabbath day.
4. Honor your father and your mother.
5. You shall not kill.
6. You shall not commit adultery.
7. You shall not steal.
8. You shall not bear false witness against your neighbor.
9. You shall not covet your neighbor's wife.
10. You shall not covet your neighbor's goods.

(See Exodus 20:1-17 and Deuteronomy 5:6-22.)

Act of Contrition
O my God, I am heartily sorry for having offended you, and I detest all my sins, because of your just punishments, but most of all because they offend you, my God, who are all good and deserving of all my love. I firmly resolve, with the help of your grace, to sin no more and to avoid the near occasions of sin. Amen.

Acts of Faith, Hope and Charity

Act of Faith
O my God, I firmly believe that you are one God in three divine Persons, Father, Son, and Holy Spirit; I believe that your divine Son became man and died for our sins, and that he shall come to judge the living and the dead. I believe these and all the truths that the holy Catholic Church teaches, because you have revealed them, who can neither deceive nor be deceived.

Act of Hope
O my God, relying on your almighty power and infinite mercy and promises, I hope to obtain pardon for my sins, the help of your grace, and life everlasting, through the merits of Jesus Christ, my Lord and Redeemer.

Act of Charity
O my God, I love you above all things, with my whole heart and soul, because you are all-good and worthy of all love. I love my neighbor as myself for the love of you. I forgive all who have injured me and ask pardon of all whom I have injured.

Stations of the Cross or Way of the Cross
(From *Catholic Family Prayer Book*, by Jacquelyn Lindsey.)

The Stations ideally are prayed in a church, moving from one Station to the next. Parents could walk with their children around the church and explain the different Stations in words appropriate for the ages of the children. There are many versions of the Stations. The following is one example.

After an introductory prayer, each station usually begins with:

V. We adore you, O Christ, and we praise you.
R. Because by your holy Cross you have redeemed the world.

At each Station, a meditation is made and a prayer may be added. Suggested texts appear after the Stations. In public devotions a verse of the Stabat Mater *is often sung after each Station.*

The First Station: Jesus is condemned to death. (Matthew 27:26; Mark 15:15; Luke 23:23-25; John 19:16)

The Second Station: Jesus is made to carry the Cross. (John 19:17)

The Third Station: Jesus falls the first time. (Matthew 27:31)

The Fourth Station: Jesus meets his Blessed Mother. (John 19:25-27)

The Fifth Station: Simon helps Jesus carry his Cross. (Matthew 27:32; Mark 15:21; Luke 23:26)

The Sixth Station: Veronica wipes the face of Jesus. (Luke 23:27)

The Seventh Station: Jesus falls the second time. (Luke 23:26)

The Eighth Station: Jesus speaks to the women of Jerusalem. (Luke 23:28-31)

The Ninth Station: Jesus falls the third time. (John 19:17)

The Tenth Station: Jesus is stripped of his garments. (Luke 23:34)

The Eleventh Station: Jesus is nailed to the Cross. (Matthew 27:33-38; Mark 15:22-27; Luke 23:33-34; John 19:18)

The Twelfth Station: Jesus dies on the Cross. (Matthew 27:46-50; Mark 15:34-37; Luke 23:46; John 19:28-30)

The Thirteenth Station: Jesus is taken down from the Cross. (Matthew 27:57-58; Mark 15:42-45; Luke 28:50-52; John 19:38)

The Fourteenth Station: Jesus is placed in the tomb. (Matthew 27:59-61; Mark 15:46-47; Luke 23:53-56; John 19:39-42)

The Fifteenth Station (optional): The Resurrection. (Matthew 28; Mark 16; Luke 24; John 20)

The Stations are usually conducted with prayers for the intentions of the Holy Father, e.g., an Our Father, Hail Mary, and Glory Be.

The Stations of the Cross is an ancient devotion brought back from the Holy Land, where pilgrims retraced the footsteps of Jesus on the road to Calvary.

About the Author

Danny Abramowicz played in the National Football League for the New Orleans Saints, from 1967 to 1973, and the San Francisco 49ers, from 1973 to 1974. He later worked as a special teams coach for the Chicago Bears and an offensive coordinator for the Saints. He is the executive director of Donum Dei, a charitable foundation in New Orleans, and he speaks to Catholic groups around the country.

Notes